In Hindsight

In Hindsight

42 Essential Things for a Life That Counts

David Hind

New Wine Press

New Wine Ministries
PO Box 17
Chichester
West Sussex
United Kingdom
PO19 2AW

Copyright © 2006 David Hind

All rights reserved. No part of this publication may be reproduced, stored in a retrieval system, or transmitted in any form or by any means, electronic, mechanical, photocopying or otherwise, without the prior written consent of the publisher. Short extracts may be used for review purposes.

Scripture quotations are taken from the following versions of the Bible:

NIV – The Holy Bible, New International Version
Copyright © 1973, 1978, 1984 by International Bible Society.
Used by permission of Hodder and Stoughton Limited.

NKJV – The Holy Bible, New King James Version
Copyright © 1982 by Thomas Nelson Inc.

ISBN 1-903725-71-2

For more information about the author see www.davidhind.co.uk

Typeset by CRB Associates, Reepham, Norfolk
Cover design by CCD, www.ccdgroup.co.uk
Back cover photo by Adrian Davies
Printed in Malta

Contents

	Dedication	7
	Acknowledgements	8
	Foreword	9
	Preface	10
1	The Operating Thing	11
2	The Memory Thing	13
3	The Rest Thing	16
4	The Miracle Thing	20
5	The Father Thing	23
6	The Wrestling Thing	26
7	The Regret Thing	29
8	The Yes, Sex After Marriage Thing	31
9	The Dad Thing	34
10	The Faith Thing	38
11	The Legacy Thing	41
12	The Love Thing	43
13	The Determination Thing	46
14	The Affair Thing	48
15	The Honour Thing	51
16	The More Thing	53
17	The Why Thing	57
18	The Loyalty Thing	60

19	The Men Thing	63
20	The Worship Thing	67
21	The Burden Thing	69
22	The Teenagers Thing	71
23	The Remember Thing	74
24	The Marriage Thing	76
25	The Lost Thing	79
26	The Serving Thing	82
27	The Musicians Thing	84
28	The No Sex Before Marriage Thing	87
29	The Words Thing	89
30	The Parenting Thing	92
31	The First Steps Thing	95
32	The Smell Thing	98
33	The Giants Thing	101
34	The Dying Thing	103
35	The Today Thing	106
36	The Hope Thing	108
37	The Children Thing	111
38	The Boundaries Thing	114
39	The Money Thing	116
40	The Running Thing	120
41	The Finishing Thing	122
42	The Reminder Thing	125

Dedication

Dedicated to the memory of my dad, Peter Hind.
25th October 1926 – 30th September 2004.

Acknowledgements

Thanks to so many people...

- Susan, the love of my life
- Sam, Tom, I couldn't be more proud of you both
- Mum, thank you for everything
- Kathryn, Janice and Teresa, you are all wonderful. Hey, your brother is an author!
- All my family, especially Stuart, Sarah and Rachel, whom I promised would be in the book!
- Rachel Bussell for giving me the little brown book that led to me writing
- David Shearman and John Pettifor who have always loved me enough to be honest
- To the team and leaders at the Christian Centre, I am proud to serve with you
- To the congregation in Nottingham, I love our church
- To Tim Pettingale who encouraged me to give it a go and opened a door for me
- To Chris, Rob and Amanda, Adrian and Lynette, who have been so generous to us
- And finally to Cerin Wilson, Sarah Woodall, Jamie Fyleman and Susan Hind who read every word, encouraged me to write better and were kind. It was great fun.

Foreword

Hello. I am Susan, David's wife and the mother of our two boys, Sam and Tom. As someone close to the author (obviously), I cannot pretend to have an unbiased opinion about this book.

What I can tell you, though, before you read it, is that it is a real book. By that I mean that it is an honest reflection of David, and it is the fruit not just of hard work writing a manuscript, but also of lessons learned in a real life.

Interestingly enough, I first met David through the written word, in a letter written to me in the week he became a Christian. I had written to him the day before, having been told of his experience with God by his mum Brenda, a friend and colleague of mine. In my own way I wanted to encourage him as he took the first steps in his new life. His reply was open, passionate and enthusiastic. It spoke of someone who had already grasped that the decision he had made would change his life forever, and who was eager to follow, as he put it, "the path of Jesus".

When I first met David a few days later, he lived up to his words. He was also immensely human and as we got to know each other better, we learned many lessons together, and not always the easy way.

David is a wonderful person to be close to: a genuine, funny, spontaneous and warm-hearted man, with a zest for life and a very real passion for his Saviour.

As you read this book, may you capture some of his heart, and be inspired by the journey so far.

Susan Hind
Nottingham, April 2006

Preface

I've heard it said that you are what you read. Therefore I should be a vet (James Herriott), a lawyer (John Grisham), a small dog (Peanuts) or a Catholic monk (Brennan Manning).

The truth is I have to work at reading. I can get bored with lengthy explanations of ideas and I long for authors to be open to write thirty pages if that explains it adequately.

Therefore I have written a book, about life, in which no chapter is long and hopefully no thought is overstated. In 128 pages you get forty-two chapters that aim to be real, provoking, and at times, moving and humorous.

All I have written has been learnt up to my fortieth year through family, church life, friendship and by making a lot of mistakes.

I don't think this is a mid-life crisis book, but I'm pretty sure the psychologists among you have me sussed already.

Anyway, I love Jesus, I love my wife and boys, I love the church and I love life. I pray you will find encouragement as you read on.

1

The Operating Thing

Other than a tonsillectomy and two minor operations I've not encountered much surgery. However, if you have struggled with tonsillitis for ten to fifteen years, then losing your tonsils is just fantastic. I will also never forget the nurse who spoke to me as I sat in a small surgical gown feeling very vulnerable before "the snip": "Oh hello, it's David Hind isn't it? We were in a production together. I'll see you in surgery!"

In October 2004 my Dad died after a short illness. He was seventy-seven. Two days before he died I sat in hospital with him, held his hand and we expressed our love for one another. I then had the privilege of preaching at his funeral and spoke of his faith in Jesus and his love for his family.

I had never faced the death of someone close to me before and following the funeral, my grief took me by surprise. Where does a Christian minister go when they need healing and to be vulnerable?

I decided to have professional counselling and during these very important sessions the counsellor simply listened and led me to the operating table where, once again, I realised my need of Jesus.

God's operating table – I've been there many times, have you?

- The time I forgave Kevin who bullied me at school.

- The time I knew God had healed me from a fear of separation that probably attacked me during the first two weeks of boarding school.
- The time when walking on Brighton beach I realised the need to forgive myself for wrong relationships and regrets from before I was a Christian.
- The many times when I have simply needed the healing hand of Jesus to sort my fragile heart out.

Many believe that to acknowledge need is a weakness, but I believe it is a strength. The Bible says, *"When I am weak, then I am strong"* (2 Corinthians 12:10). Some believe that one prayer at conversion is enough to "sort everything out", and in one sense it is, but the appropriation of this prayer seems to take a little longer.

Recently I heard a phrase that has helped me: "We are all damaged goods in recovery." Well, I have been damaged and I am in recovery, but I find the healing process is worth the effort.

Some people are kept away from God's operating table by their theology, their pride, or their fears, but listen:

- God loved you even before He created the world.
- You are a precious, planned, unique and special person.
- You are welcome to come to Him whenever you like.
- God already knows your failings and needs, and you do not embarrass Him.
- His operating table is always available; there is never a waiting list and no time limit.
- No pain is too hard for Him; no oppressive force too great for Him to overcome; no regret or mistake unforgivable.

Come as you are to God's operating table, be healed and then go and change the world.

2
The Memory Thing

For anyone who doesn't know, *Top Trumps* is a card game whereby the aim is to collect all the cards in the pack. The subject matter varies, but whether it is sports cars or film characters, relative strengths and weaknesses are given a rating and when pitted against your opponent, the best rating wins.

At ten years old Thomas, my youngest son, decided to make a pack of *Top Trump* cards based on the staff at his junior school. He drew pictures, allocated points for strengths/weaknesses, coolness (and, unfortunately, the opposite) and recorded each teacher's "special attack" method. Tragically a member of staff discovered the cards and so it was that all the staff gathered around a table to learn their nicknames, discover who was the "heaviest" and what were the weaknesses that the boys talked about. I'm glad they saw the funny side.

On another occasion, we were invited to have tea with a neighbour who kept pets and I had spent much time instructing Samuel, my eldest son, not to draw attention to the overwhelming "hamster smell" I knew would greet us as we arrived. He agreed and so we knocked on the door. Samuel said, "Hello", walked in, sniffed loudly, and said to our neighbour, "Mmm, what a lovely smell!"

Memories are powerful

Memories link you to moments in your history and are often the first things you recall when you get together with friends you haven't seen for a while. My dear friend Malcolm, who now leads a church in South Africa and who has always been a huge support in my life, left me so many memories that make me smile. He arrived at the hospital to see us almost before Samuel had been born. At thirty-eight years old he hid in a cupboard in his office when I went to see him, leaving just his shoes on the windowsill. After an all night prayer meeting in Burkina Faso he preached to a congregation in which dozens of people were soundly asleep. For months afterwards he tried to convince me that it was a local custom, if people were enjoying a message, to put their head in their hands.

Memories are humorous

For me there are so many...

- The time when Samuel put his head under a lady's cubicle at the swimming baths to tell her, "I can see you."
- Thomas on the back of his mum's bike travelling to nursery. At the hills he would say, "Come on Mummy, faster, you can do it!"
- Samuel spitting on the conveyor belt at the supermarket checkout to watch it go round and round.
- The question asked of me by a nurse in casualty after a serious groin strain: "Would you like the small, medium or large support Mr Hind?"

Memories are retold

What did Peter say later when he spoke of seeing Elijah and Moses on the mountain? What did the little girl say when asked to explain what Jesus' face looked like when He raised her from the dead?

What did the servant say when he described how Jesus made his ear grow again in the garden of Gethsemane?

Memories can be painful

They can link you to a moment when you hoped things would have been different.

Finally, making memories should be planned

Some memories simply happen as part of life and you enjoy them. But some memories have to be planned. As an individual, and as a family, make the most of every moment. Here are a few possibilities:

- Climb a mountain
- Do something for the first time
- Save up and travel to a country in the developing world
- Eat in a great restaurant
- Give away something that you really like

We have one go at life and living with yesterday's regrets will only harm tomorrow's possibilities. Make the most of every opportunity and seize every day. It doesn't have to cost a penny, but the time investment in making a memory can be priceless.

Make a memory today.

3

The Rest Thing

I am writing this on a day when I am tired. This week I have been over busy and this has meant less sleep than normal. Added to this, on Sunday night our burglar alarm went off at midnight and I rushed downstairs shouting, "Hello?" to anyone who may be helping themselves to our possessions. I was comforted by the thought that my lads would be down in a flash if a fight ensued. With the alarm eventually turned off, the house checked and silence restored, all I could hear was the sound of my boys, soundly sleeping, not having even stirred.

When the same thing happened the very next night, I decided to "poke around" with a screwdriver in one of the sensors. The whole alarm fused (costing me £170) and the alarm bell rang out for longer than I am emotionally able to face telling you. When the emergency call-out man arrived at 1.30am he reversed at high speed into a lamp post outside our house. When he eventually prised open the boot of his car, his car alarm sounded and he loudly greeted my already suffering neighbours with language I haven't heard in too many Christian choruses!

Life is a lot easier to face after a good night's sleep!

I recently went to see Thomas while he was working in our computer room. He was communicating with around eight people on MSN Messenger, listening to music, had the television on, and at the same time he was trying to text someone on his mobile phone, peel an orange and do his homework! I jest not! Call minding, conference calls, email, mobile phones, coffee in a travel cup, multi-tasking. Is there no end to things that seek to rob us of a little rest?

Now, I believe in hard work and that every adult is called to be a "working" person. For some this may mean working in the home, for others it is working outside the home, but we are all called to work hard. I also believe that every Christian is called to serve in their local church. Churches suffer from too many self-seeking Christians who can worship with passion, but then not serve, pick up litter, or make time to help others.

So when you consider all this, how does the rest thing work?

- Rest was built into the natural rhythm of life by God. He rested on the seventh day after creating the world and mankind.
- Rest draws boundaries around work and gives us chance to celebrate what we have achieved.
- Rest brings refreshment and re-orientates our values.
- Rest sets a pattern for life. Jesus said, "Come with me by yourself to a quiet place and get some rest" (see Matthew 11:28).
- Rest is the promise of God.

So, a few keys to find rest that I am finding helpful . . .

Learn the secret of contentment

In his fantastic book, *Ordering Your Private World*,[1] Gordon MacDonald talks about driven people.

1. A driven person is most often gratified only by accomplishment and its symbols.

2. A driven person is usually caught in the uncontrolled pursuit of expansion.
3. Driven people tend to have a limited regard for integrity and are easily angered.
4. Driven people are usually abnormally busy and highly competitive.

I love to achieve, push things forward and dream of growth, but I don't want to be a driven man and the balance is not always easy to find. Contentment is a key to rest and Paul writes, *"I know what it is to be in need, and I know what it is to have plenty. I have learned the secret of being content in any and every situation, whether well fed or hungry, whether living in plenty or in want"* (Philippians 4:12). Have you learned the secret?

Watch how you live

You are precious and you need to look after yourself. A healthy diet, drinking lots of water, observing wise bedtimes, getting regular exercise, having structured time when you are quiet, and plenty of laughter are all important.

Maintain healthy relationships

Honouring marriage and friendship is healthy. If you say sorry, forgive regularly and practise loyalty you will find it easier to rest.

Like yourself

If you live with skeletons in the cupboard of your life, then rest is hard to find. Have a "clear out", live in the light and realise you are amazing.

Be secure and trust Him for everything

Lean on God, hold onto Him, rely on Him and walk with Him. Everything is alright.

Live close to Jesus

If you walk close to Jesus you will be a more restful person.

Jesus said, *"Come to me, all you who are weary and burdened, and I will give you rest"* (Matthew 11:28).

Note
1. Gordon MacDonald, *Ordering Your Private World*, Highland Books, 2003.

4

The Miracle Thing

On a Friday afternoon Susan and I sat in a consultant's room at Nottingham City Hospital. The professor with us began to explain the diagnosis of Samuel's condition, which we had suspected for some time. The implications were massive as there was no cure, and whilst we would have support, there would be no solution. As we sat there we were grateful for the honesty of the hospital, but unaware of the journey that would take place over the coming years.

Samuel was statemented and given special educational support in nursery and early schooling. At eight years old he moved to a Christian school, eventually leaving at sixteen to begin his career. Since we sat in the professor's room there have been countless stories that one day may be written. There have been many tears, much frustration, private battles, huge lessons learnt and a grace from God to see a miracle. We have always felt it was a privilege to have Samuel and our lives have been richer because of him.

Today Samuel has gone to work where he is being trained and is living a completely normal life. He is fun, hard working, communicative and a strong Christian. He is a miracle. As we see Samuel doing and being many things that his diagnosis predicted would be impossible, we look back on what have been the keys for our miracle. There have been some specific steps.

Prayer

We prayed for Samuel before he was born, we sang to him in the womb, prayed over him the promises of God and expected him to be blessed. When we received the diagnosis we asked two of the Elders from our church to come to our house and anoint Samuel with oil. We prayed that from that moment he would begin to be healed and since then, almost day-by-day, Samuel has changed. His educational statement was removed, he improved beyond recognition, and he is now a healthy, handsome young man.

Promise

The Samuel of the Bible knew the presence of God, the favour of God, heard the voice of God, and knew how to speak the words of God. We have prayed similar promises over Samuel on probably thousands of occasions. We believe that God said to us that Samuel would grow in stature and in favour with God and man. This is true of him now and we believe will continue to be true of him in the future.

Consistency

Although we have made allowances, we have always expected high standards of Samuel. We have insisted, held our ground and brought loving discipline to him. Alongside this, Susan in particular has worked for hours to help Samuel be the man he is today.

Support

We are blessed with hugely supportive parents and families who have helped us, prayed for us and stood with us. People at church have been there for us and we have known overwhelming love from other Christians.

Grace

Samuel is a miracle. His healing is a gift from God. For that we are forever grateful.

Perhaps you need a miracle today and perhaps the wait has been longer than you anticipated.

Take courage and never forget,

- Whatever you are faced with, God is not overwhelmed.
- The miraculous is still promised today. God is able and prayer changes things.

Miracles come from God. Never stop asking Him and believe you will see your miracle.

5

The Father Thing

I am standing in the NEC Birmingham with over 11,000 others and as I look at Samuel, I realise that though this may not be my first choice of entertainment, this moment with my son is priceless. Therefore I listen, smile and muse on whether there are any other Christian ministers at this Iron Maiden concert – you never know!

I am standing beside the grave of a five-year-old boy in Northern Ghana – the only son in his family – and Thomas and I have a different, yet equally significant moment. Joseph had died because he was given a wrong prescription for malaria. The dosage had killed him, unnecessarily. The father next to me loved his son and we capture his pain.

The word "father" evokes so many emotions. For some it is the pain of never *being* a father, though they long to be. For others it is the memories of a dad no longer alive; for others wonderful memories; and still others, the feeling of disappointment. Whether the word stimulates images of protection or vulnerability we all carry these feelings about our earthly fathers with us as we explore the concept of God being our Father.

How we were loved and accepted has an impact on us. If your father was mean, absent or unfaithful you can believe, wrongly, that God will be equally unreliable and your Christian growth will be stunted. Yet, one of the greatest revelations in the Bible is that of God as the perfect Father: *"'I will be a Father to you, and you will be my sons and daughters,' says the Lord Almighty"* (2 Corinthians 6:18).

So what does the Father bring to you?

He brings acceptance

Low self-esteem is a problem for so many people because we don't realise how important we are to God. "When we grasp that as children of God he is interested in us, is never too busy for us and that he desires a direct and personal relationship with us we discover self-worth."[1] Affirmation and security come from the Father.

He brings involvement

God is able to watch over 6 billion people at the same time without feeling overwhelmed. He knows everything about each person and is available to any one of us 24 hours a day. Both the Bible and psychologists agree that a person cannot answer the question, "Who am I?" without knowing who his or her father is. When you truly grasp and know that God is your Father, you no longer have an identity problem.

He brings love and affection

God loves us because He loves us and as our Father He will never stop loving us.

He brings lavishness

Creation shows the sheer complexity of God. The creatures that live at the bottom of the deepest oceans, never seen by anyone, are there for God's enjoyment and an example of His generosity. To know that He longs to lavish us with His goodness is immense.

He brings faithfulness

Before we were born, even before the creation of the world, God knew us and was waiting for us. In life He will never leave us or forsake us and in death He has gone ahead of us and will return to take us to be with Him.

I recently asked my boys whether I am a good Dad. Thomas said, "You're great as long as you don't dress too young!" Samuel said, "Dad you are rubbish and don't ask stupid questions." I think therefore, I'm probably doing OK! The Father though, is always wonderful, always perfect and always completely trustworthy.

Father God accepts you and wants to be involved with your life. He loves you, wants to lavish His goodness on you and will be faithful to you forever.

Note
1. Derek Prince, *Husbands and Fathers*, Sovereign World, 2000.

6

The Wrestling Thing

On Saturday afternoons as a boy I used to watch the ITV World of Sport wrestling show. Characters like Big Daddy, Giant Haystacks and others used to grapple, bounce and hurt each other and we all believed (well I did!) that it was for real. Being a spectator of manufactured TV wrestling is one thing, but we rarely anticipate the wrestling matches that life itself draws us into.

In June 2002, Susan and I went on a weekend break to Cambridge. It was to be a romantic, sightseeing, meals out and (in my head), phenomenal sex sort of weekend. During the Saturday afternoon, whilst we were walking, I developed a chronic back pain that got worse and worse to the point where I could hardly breathe. I was admitted into Addenbrooke's Hospital and closely examined for a potential punctured lung, heart attack, blood clot or cancer. After a few days, a CT scan and further tests I was released and told that a viral infection had gone through my body. I was troubled by this and felt drawn to read about Jacob wrestling with God.

I realised that I was becoming restless and impatient with my life and, I believe, over these few days I was actually wrestling with God about it. I had to decide whether I would truly trust Him, rely on His timing and believe that He, having made the universe and sustaining it with His love, was able to look after me. I came to a new point of yielding to God and it was hugely beneficial.

Now this is the tough part to write: I've told this story, toured around the country with an album containing a song about this moment and used my experience to help others. However, I've been in for a couple more rounds of wrestling since. I know God *still loves* me, is able to open and close doors for me and is not overwhelmed by the task of leading me. I believe again that if I am faithful and obey Him, the will of God will find me.

Here are some lessons I learnt and am learning from Genesis 32:22–32.

When you wrestle with God you will do it on your own (vv. 22–24)

Real faith has to be personally lived out. For Jacob the conflict brought to a head the battling and struggling of a lifetime. Jacob's methods didn't work and he had to yield, on his own, to the Master's plan – it's the same for us.

When you wrestle with God you will yield your possessions (vv. 23–24)

When I preached on this, I stood in the offering basket as a picture of what God wants from me.

Does God require my substance? *Yes*

Does He want to be in charge of all my resources? *Yes*

However, He wants something more. *Jesus wants me!*

When you wrestle with God you have to persevere (v. 24)

David found strength in God and encouraged himself. Nehemiah found out the facts and then re-envisioned the people. Jesus wrestled in the night and then prayed, *"Not my will, but yours be done."* If you are wrestling don't give up, hold on, there is a blessing ahead.

When you wrestle with God you receive a blessing (vv. 25, 26–29)

I love Jacob's words, *"I will not let you go unless you bless me."* For Jacob, the blessing this time was not contrived and was untarnished. To break through the desire to have your will and to embrace instead, His will, and walk before the living God dependent on Him, is the essence of *real* blessing.

When you wrestle with God you walk differently (vv. 25–31)

Jacob's fighting turned to dependence and he emerged broken and blessed. His limp was lasting proof of the reality of the struggle. When you wrestle with God, people will know you have been with Jesus: you will have a different walk, a greater peace, a stronger contentment and a greater desire for Him.

I can't guarantee it will be over in one round, but the struggle is worth it.

7
The Regret Thing

Susan and I married in Bar Hill church in Cambridge. I have almost no memories of the day other than the fact that Susan looked wonderful and my tie was bright green. I am told that the photographer had to continually tell me to smile less, so I imagine I looked happy!

As Susan walked down the aisle I realised that she was a rose from God, saved for me. I was Susan's first boyfriend – the only man she has ever kissed – and she brought to me the gift of her virginity. For this I was, and am, very grateful. At our wedding I could not bring the same gift to Susan and although I was forgiven, and we had talked of my life before I met her, I regretted this. In fact, this remains the biggest regret of my life. I can't change it and I don't blame anyone else for it, I simply regret it.

I have just watched an episode of the *West Wing*, which has triggered this chapter. The *West Wing* is my favourite TV series ever and I love it. In the episode I have just watched, the female press secretary is looking back at a relationship she wishes had never happened...

"There is no night of my life I regret more than that one. I wish I could explain it. If I could take back one moment of my life, it would be then."

People carry so many regrets in life. I have talked to people who regret having an abortion, regret a relationship, regret their part in a failed marriage and regret financial mistakes. Others regret a decision that caused devastation and regret not expressing love when they had the opportunity. The list could go on of the many things we would do differently, if only there was a second chance.

As Peter saw Jesus on the shore after the resurrection, I believe his emotions were in turmoil. The joy of seeing the One he loved, and the regret that he had betrayed Him, was real for Peter. As he reached the shore he would have looked into the eyes that accepted him and believed in him and he carried the regret that those same eyes had seen him deny and walk away. Three times Peter denied Jesus and three times Jesus spoke to him on the beach.

Jesus said to Peter, *"Do you love me? . . . follow me!"* (John 21:17, 19).

Jesus gave Peter a second chance.

So the regret thing, how do we move on?

- Be honest with yourself and bring your regrets into the open. It can be good to confess your sins to someone else.
- Ask Jesus to forgive you – He will. *"Godly sorrow brings repentance that leads to salvation and leaves no regret"* (2 Corinthians 7:10).
- If you have wronged another and they are still alive, talk to them, write to them, or find a way to apologise.
- Forgive yourself and start again.
- Receive and be amazed by the grace of God that gives you a second chance.

Look forward – this is a new day.

8
The Yes, Sex After Marriage Thing

When Neil Armstrong first walked on the moon, as well as his "one small step for man, one giant step for mankind" statement, he made a number of other comments, including the remark, "Good luck, Mr Gorsky!"

Over the years many people asked Armstrong what this statement meant, but he would never give an answer. However on 5th July, 1995, at the end of an interview, he was asked again about the twenty-six year old statement. This time he felt he could answer as Mr Gorsky was now dead.

When he was a child he was playing baseball with a friend when his friend hit the ball and it landed in front of his neighbour's bedroom windows. His neighbours were Mr and Mrs Gorsky.

As he leaned down to get the ball, he heard Mrs Gorsky shouting at Mr Gorsky, "Sex! You want sex? You'll get sex when the kid next door walks on the moon!"[1]

Our honeymoon was not the textbook fortnight you dream about. However, it wasn't as bad as the honeymoon of a friend of mine who, arriving at the hotel late on his wedding night, was determined to make the most of the moment, even though it was 2.00am.

Afterwards, his wife's response to him was a reality check: "Is that it? Is that all there is to sex!"

Arriving back in church as the new youth workers, everyone wanted to know how Susan and I were. I decided that the response should not be, "Thanks for asking, but the sex is not working and we are both cheesed off. Anyway, how are you?" So we smiled, said "thank you" and carried on. Our challenge continued for around six months, during which time we loved one another, but intercourse didn't happen. We never asked for help and we were too proud and embarrassed to be vulnerable.

We are now in our twentieth year of marriage and without meaning to be crude, sex is great! We have since talked to couples that have had, or have, similar challenges to us, and face either no sex, or unsatisfying sex and frustration.

So, a few points:

Sex is good, created by God, and a gift to every married couple

Don't over spiritualise your physical relationship. You don't have to pray before sex; it is not a sin to enjoy it and it's fine to experiment together.

Sex is a journey that is meant to get better and better

Discovering how another person is designed is part of the joy of marriage. Making mistakes together brings knowledge which, if remembered, can lead to better things.

Great sex comes from consideration, appreciation and other person centredness

The secret of great sex is in not doing anything that the other person doesn't like. The key is to find ways of showing your love to them. Self-centredness and selfishness will spoil the physical side of your marriage and probably much more.

It's alright to ask for advice

I believe that if we remain teachable and pliable we can only get better. If you are struggling in your physical relationship together then find another couple you respect and, in confidence, ask them for some advice.

Is it possible for two people to be together for a lifetime, enjoy sex and never betray that love with another?

I believe, yes.

Have fun!

Note
1. J. John and Mark Stibbe, *A Box of Delights*, Monarch, 2001.

9
The Dad Thing

Nothing prepared me for the joy and challenge of being a Dad. It has been, without doubt, the steepest learning curve of my life. As a youth leader I felt able to "teach" parents with the wisdom I had acquired through *not* having children. Now I'm in an entirely different category and I need the youth leader to teach me! I am proud of my boys and, of course, biased towards them. I will give them a hug, kiss them, and tell them I love them until my dying day. Their only request is that I don't do it in front of their mates!

It has been my experience that many men don't know what to do with their children. They don't know how to relate to them, how to enter their world, how to resolve conflict and bring discipline. I've never brought up a girl, so hopefully the following will work for boys *and* girls. From one learner Dad to another, here are my top 11 "do's" for Dads:

1. Get yourself sorted out

So many Dads never come to terms with their own upbringing, which for all of us was imperfect. Perhaps you have never known your real Dad; maybe you were told that you were unplanned; perhaps as a child you were never hugged, encouraged or loved, or worse still you were abused? Listen, with respect, *so what?* The experiences you have lived through so far need not limit the potential of the rest of your life. Seek God, get healed, forgive quickly, sort out your baggage, and don't pass your rubbish on to your children. Despite the challenges you have faced in the past you can be a great Dad in the future.

2. Love your wife

One of the greatest gifts you can give your children is to love their Mum. If children see their parents being affectionate to one another, expressing love and working through differences, they will learn to do that too. Be romantic, generous and express your love to your family.

3. Realise you will make mistakes

You can never be a perfect father, so be quick to say sorry when you make a mistake and don't dwell on the past. I remember apologising for the second time to my son Thomas for a mistake I had made. He said to me, "Not that again Dad! We've dealt with that, move on!"

4. Pray for them

Last night I stood in our boys' bedrooms and prayed out loud the promises God has given us for them – something Sue and I have done thousands of times. Let your children know you pray for them. At bedtime go into their rooms and bring them before God. Also, there is no example more powerful than if they wake up in the morning to the sound of you praying in another room.

5. Train them

At the time of my Dad's death we realised that we, his children, had inherited many of his gifts and tastes. Whilst there was an element of overlap, I had Dad's love of music, Kathryn had his love of nature, Janice had his love of literature and Teresa had his love of creativity and art. Teach your children what you know. It won't be long until they begin to teach you! Whenever you think of something they don't know, teach them and remember: they learn most by watching your life.

6. Talk to them

If you read your kids stories when they are young and chat to them about your life, when they need to they will come and talk to you about issues that bother them or they don't understand. The big conversations about life and sex, and the everyday conversations seeking advice or facing challenges, will happen mostly when they are ready if you model the example of an open life. Don't be embarrassed and never make them feel stupid, no matter what they ask you. I have been asked just about every question imaginable by my boys: "Were you a virgin before you met mum?"; "Did you and mum sleep together before you were married?"; "Have you ever been in debt?" etc.!

7. Trust them

This is a challenge and I am still learning. As a parent you have to put secure boundaries in place. Make wise decisions with issues such as giving children TVs in their bedrooms, giving them access to the Internet, regarding girlfriends and boyfriends, bedtime and pocket money. Realise that one day they will make their decisions for themselves and it's a good idea to allow them to make some choices, make a few mistakes and have a few successes whilst they are still at home.

8. Be fun to be with

I still find breaking wind very funny and many times, to Sue's slight disapproval, we boys have laughed and laughed about it. Laugh, tell stories, do exciting things, be spontaneous, generous and don't take yourself too seriously.

9. Enter their lives

Don't try and be like your kids, that's just embarrassing, but do everything you can to approve of their lives whenever they choose to let you in. They may give you fashion advice, "Dad that shirt is too young for you, and your hair is looking strange!", but don't give them the same advice unless they are open to it – trust me on this one! When they talk to you, listen first, think second, speak third, and always be available. Children quickly work out if you are really there for them or merely fitting them into your schedule. I tell my boys that if they really need me they can interrupt anything I am doing at any time.

10. Ask for help

I'm a learner and so are you. Find other Dads you trust and ask for their wisdom and advice. What mistakes did they make, how did they build good relationships and how did they put an effective discipline structure in place?

11. Leave them a legacy

If you haven't done it already, make a will, get advice and plan for the future. Leave your children an inheritance and give them a balanced and exciting perspective on the life of faith. Teach them how to give financially to God and always, always, love them – no matter what happens.

You can be a great Dad and everything will be alright!

10

The Faith Thing

In 1996 a Christian ministry grew in southern England, which was dedicated to helping people. In 1999 they believed God spoke to them saying He would lead them to a resource centre called, "The House of Bread" and that the leaders would have to have all things in common. Over the following months they tried to find the place God had spoken of and all sold their houses in preparation. Three times they nearly bought venues and Elizabeth (one of the leaders) found herself in a bed and breakfast hotel near Brecon preparing to view another property the next morning.

During the night she had a dream and in the dream she saw a house with pink stones and a clear stained glass window. She then heard God say, "The place you have come to see is not in Brecon, rather drive to Monmouth [40 miles away] and find a statue in the centre. Behind the statue there is an estate agent. Go in and tell them you have come to buy the House of Bread." At nine o'clock the next morning she found the statue and estate agent, entered the property and said, "We have come to buy the House of Bread." The estate agent said, "If we did have such a property what do you want it for?" Elizabeth then told them about the dream, the pink stones, the stained glass window and described their need for three dwellings, a meeting room, and told the estate agent how much money they had to pay.

The estate agent then told her that in 1752 a special property had been built as a bakehouse with three dwellings, known as the House of Bread, with pink stones. A unique stained glass window was added in 1992 at the front. It had enough rooms for all their needs. Also they would have £5,000 of their budget left over for decorations etc. On 15th May 2002, just two months after this conversation, they moved in. Since then over 5,000 people have been helped, found faith, received healing, and been encouraged in this place.

In the unseen journey of waiting, questioning and "what ifs?", God is faithful.

Faith, for me, is a day-by-day journey as I aim to believe Him more and trust Him with everything. At times I can believe God for anything; at others I am at best like the man who met Jesus and said, "I do believe; help me overcome my unbelief!" (Mark 9:24).

So how can we grow in faith?

By receiving faith from the Word of God

The Bible is the best inspirer of faith. *"Faith comes by hearing, and hearing by the word of God"* (Romans 10:17 NKJV).

By receiving faith from Bible characters

There are so many inspiring Bible characters. In Hebrews 11 we read,

> *"I do not have time to tell about* [those] *who through faith conquered kingdoms, administered justice, and gained what was promised; who shut the mouths of lions, quenched the fury of the flames, and escaped the edge of the sword ... God had planned something better for us..."*
>
> (Hebrews 11:32–34, 40)

By receiving faith from history

Whatever has been thrown at the Christian Church for the last two thousand years, it has continued to grow and offer hope to the world. If you read of Smith Wigglesworth, Billy Graham, George

Müller, and Mother Theresa, they all had their challenges, but found faith in a faithful God.

I love this extract from the journal of John Wesley:

Sunday May 5th am	Preached in St Ann's. Was asked not to come back any more.
Sunday May 5th pm	Preached in St John's. Deacons said, "Get out and stay out."
Sunday May 12th am	Preached in St Jude's. Can't go back there either.
Sunday May 19th pm	Preached on street; kicked off street.
Sunday May 26th am	Preached in meadow. Chased out of meadow by a bull that was set on us.
Sunday June 2nd am	Preached out at the edge of town. Kicked off the highway.
Sunday June 2nd pm	Preached in a pasture. Ten thousand people came out to hear me.[1]

By receiving faith from your story

If you are reading this book as a Christian, stop and remember the goodness, kindness, mercy and love of God to you. Where would you be without Jesus?

If you are reading and are on a journey to faith, remember this. God knew you before you were conceived and created you to be filled with His presence.

Take courage from the Word of God; take courage from the journey and lives of Bible characters; take courage from history and take courage from your story.

You will grow in this "faith thing".

Note
1. John Wesley, Percy L. Parker, *The Journal of John Wesley*, Moody Publishers, 1951, paraphrased from the original.

11

The Legacy Thing

My Uncle Keith died when I was eleven years old. I remember he drove a yellowy-green Austin Princess and came every Saturday for tea when we always ate egg and chips followed by meringues and cream (I don't think we had heard of cholesterol then!). Most of all though, I remember he had a colour television and for a number of years my Dad and I would go to his house to watch the FA Cup final.

We all carry memories of people who have influenced our lives. As a teenager I loved many things, especially the band Big Country and James Herriott's books. On Sunday, 16th December 2001, the forty-three-year-old lead singer and guitarist of Big Country, Stuart Adamson, hung himself in a hotel room. On 28th June 1995, Donald Sinclair, the person upon whom the character of Siegfried Farnon in the Herriott books was based, died of an overdose. Whatever they achieved in life, I now cannot forget how they died.

What are the things you remember about people? I remember the man in the *Guinness Book of Records* who sat in a bath of beans and sausages for 146 hours. I don't remember his name, just the beans! I remember Anna who became a Christian listening to my music, a few weeks before she died of leukaemia aged fifteen.

One day people will remember certain things about you and me.

My prayer is that they say the following about David Hind:

He was a man who served God in his generation
May it be said that I knew God for myself, gave Him access to my life and ultimately did what He wanted, regardless of the cost.

He was a wonderful husband
May it be said that I always loved and stayed faithful to Susan.

He was a great father
May it be said that I did the best for my children and gave them the opportunity to stand on my shoulders and be everything they could be.

He was a faithful man who finished what he started
May it be said that I was faithful in what God gave me to do and could always be relied upon to see things through to completion.

He was a man of integrity, honesty and Christlike character
May it be said that people saw Jesus in me.

He was a generous man who gave all he could to the church, the poor and to others
May it be said that I had the grace of giving.

He was a man who loved Jesus and loved people
What will they say about you?

12

The Love Thing

I was involved in a concert in Nottingham when I received a phone call from a friend. He told me that Susan was about to give birth and I had to rush to the hospital. Now, I knew she was pregnant, but it was a month early and a doctor had told Susan, that morning, that the stomach cramps she had been experiencing were due to a urine infection.

When I arrived at the hospital, Sue was surrounded by green cloths and she was giving birth. Soon after I arrived a foot appeared and the birth was to be a breach. When I saw tiny toes and a little leg, I grasped again the fact that humanity is amazing. Samuel is now 6ft 2ins and still growing, but then he was miniscule, and as he was being born, his first act was to wee on the doctor. We had loved him from when we knew Susan was pregnant. We had talked to him, prayed over him, sung to him, and listened to him, but when we first saw him and named him Samuel, we really loved him.

So this love thing – what is it all about?

Clifford Hill tells the story of a walk on a mountainside in Abelboden, Switzerland. He had been watching the World Cup men's downhill ski event and, along with thousands of others, was making his way down the mountain. The pathway turned a sharp bend around the mountain and beyond a low wooden guardrail was a steep slope for about 100 feet to the edge of a precipice and a sheer 500 foot drop onto rocks. As he turned the corner he heard the piercing scream of a child who had fallen under the rail and was sliding to her death. As he watched, a man leapt over the rail and ran down the slope, just managed to stop before he went over the edge, and then turned and caught the little girl. As Clifford watched this scene God spoke to him, "You saw how that child was sliding to certain destruction. You saw how she looked to her father and cried for her father. You saw how her father responded immediately, not hesitating to assess the danger to himself, but flung himself down the mountainside to rescue his child? That is how I love my children ... Tell my people I love them."[1]

The love of Jesus is the most staggering example of the Father's commitment to us.

Jesus' love is demonstrated

Jesus washed feet, He touched lepers and He spoke to the marginalised and the insignificant. He had time for the dirty and the needy and the outcasts. He helped the mentally unstable and the spiritually unclean. He loved the rich and the poor and He had time for lost people. He is irresistible.

Jesus' love is unconditional

Nothing we do can make Him love us more; nothing we do can make Him love us less. His love is unconditional, undeserved and cannot be earned.

Jesus' love is eternal

He will always love us. Paul writes, *"For I am convinced that ... [nothing] in all creation, will be able to separate us from the love of God that is in Christ Jesus our Lord"* (Romans 8:38–39).

Jesus' love is compelling

He spent His three years of ministry forgiving, healing, transforming, and restoring people. One day we will see Him and He will be even more wonderful than we ever imagined.

Jesus' love is immeasurable

His love is wide and long and high and deep. His love *"surpasses knowledge"* (Ephesians 3:19).

Jesus' love is manifested by His death

The cross was painful, cursed and the greatest symbol of love the universe has ever seen. *"This is how we know what love is: Jesus Christ laid down his life for us"* (1 John 3:16).

Jesus' love is to be known

We can know Him, we can receive His love and then we can show His love to others.

The challenge for Christians to love is immense. We are to love impartially, unselfishly, sincerely and fervently. We cannot do this on our own, we must receive His love.

When I consider His unconditional, eternal, compelling, immeasurable, manifested and demonstrated love, I bow down and give my all to Him.

Note
1. Clifford Hill, *Tell My People I Love Them*, Fount paperbacks, 1983.

13
The Determination Thing

Becoming an MP at the age of twenty-one and truly finding a Christian faith at around twenty-five, William Wilberforce began to receive a burden to abolish slavery. At twenty-eight he stood almost alone in his convictions and faced huge opposition from royalty, business, parliamentary colleagues and the forces of evil. He suffered in his health, his emotions and his reputation. Yet his cry was, "Let the consequences be what they are. I determine to never rest until I have effected the abolition of slavery."

Twenty years of endless campaigning led to an initial bill being passed in the House of Commons. It took twenty-six more years to get to the point where the House of Commons passed a law to emancipate all the slaves in Britain's colonies. Wilberforce learned of it just three days before he died. He had persevered for forty-seven years. The day before John Wesley fell into a coma and died, he spoke to Wilberforce and said, "Unless God has raised you up for this very thing you will be worn out by the opposition of men and demons. But if God be for you – who can be against you?" Wilberforce never gave up and it was said at his death that his name was the greatest in the land. He was an example of determination.

There is a clear difference between godly determination and stubbornness. I remember watching Thomas learn to ride a bike without stabilisers. He was determined and unwilling to give up until, with bruised knees, he finally learnt. This is very different from the times he has dug his heels in over things in which he was wrong.

If we want to change the world we need a determined spirit, the humility to learn and yet the tenacity to never give up.

Some Christians have a dream and a "call" that seems to change very quickly when faced with challenge and difficulty. It's amazing how we think the phrase, "I feel God has said..." can justify carnality, bad character and a lack of willingness to finish what we have started. When I was a youth leader I felt it was time for a new challenge and then read in the Bible,

> "Last year you were the first not only to give but also to have the desire to do so. Now finish the work, so that your eager willingness to do it may be matched by your completion of it..."
>
> (2 Corinthians 8:10–11)

I immediately threw myself again into youth work.

I love commitment. I love people who are determined and I respect people who won't give up. It can be irresistible to meet people who believe with passion and are truly prepared to give their lives to godly causes. My brother-in-law, John, has a passion to reach lost people – a passion that has caused him to learn many languages, turn his back on a potentially prosperous career and spend his life with some of the poorest people on earth. He is a determined man.

When you look back at your life what is the pattern that you see?

- Do you easily give up?
- Are you truly committed to follow and finish Jesus' plan for your life?
- Are you determined or stubborn?

Whatever the answers, make a choice today to remain teachable and be determined.

14

The Affair Thing

I love my wife with everything I am and yet I am vulnerable. I find the thought of sexual betrayal abhorrent and nauseating and yet I am capable of it. I have watched as Christians have convinced themselves that it is alright to leave small children and a faithful husband or wife because they want sex with someone else. I have urged them to reconsider and implored them to seek help and yet, without God's help, I could do the same thing.

Don't be anxious about me or over concerned, I'm just realistic about the temptation. Recently I heard about a friend who decided that marriage, young children, the ministry and a good church were not enough – the need for an illicit relationship was more attractive. Whenever such a tragedy occurs families are blown apart, hearts broken, children deeply scarred and most of all the name of Christ is dishonoured. Is any orgasm worth this? The sex may be great, for now at least, but ultimately you will always regret affairs and betrayal.

Some marriages are challenging, but with help they can improve. In a sexless or difficult relationship a husband or wife may reach a point of desperation, but with faith there is always hope. Nothing is too difficult for God and He is able to change any heart, any situation and overcome any marital challenges. An affair is never the solution.

Think about this:

- If I sleep with another person I bring shame to the name of Christ
- If I sleep with another person I betray the promises I made to my spouse before God
- If I sleep with another person I will damage my children
- If I sleep with another person I will damage my wider family
- If I sleep with another person I will damage other Christians
- If I sleep with another person I could lose everything in my life
- If I sleep with another person my ministry ends with no guarantee of a second chance
- If I sleep with another person I will, without doubt, regret it
- If I sleep with another person I can be forgiven, but the road to recovery is long and painful

Make your own list of the names of people you would have to tell if you had an affair. Picture your Mum and Dad, picture your children, picture friends and acquaintances (some of whom you may have witnessed to) and picture your husband or wife whose life will be devastated because you have said to them, *"You were not enough for me."*

Rob Parsons puts it so powerfully as he imagines a scene in a home when an affair breaks up a marriage: "And now he stands in the hall of his home, suitcases in his hand. His daughter stands with his wife and they watch him in unbelief as if a play is unfolding. He says, 'I never meant to hurt you all.'"[1]

- *If* you are tempted to have an affair, or are in serious danger right now, call a trusted friend and ask them to pray with you. Be prepared to talk to your partner and get honest in your marriage.
- *If* you already are involved in an affair of the heart, get help, because it is only a matter of time before you ruin your life.

- *If* you have already fallen, it's not too late. To confess is always better than to be found out. The road ahead may be hard, but you still have hope.

And a word to those who in reading this know they have fallen, but believe they are "safe" from being discovered.

> "God will not be mocked and your life is in danger; nobody will get away with anything."
>
> (paraphrase of Galatians 6:7)

The affair thing is real and powerful, but you and I don't need to be part of it.

Note
1. Rob Parsons, *The Sixty Minute Marriage*, Hodder & Stoughton Ltd, 1997.

15
The Honour Thing

I came to work in ministry with David Shearman in 1987. David has been the senior leader of the Christian Centre, Nottingham since 1977 and after a year's internship, he offered me a position as the youth leader. I think there was some nervousness from the eldership as I was young, inexperienced, a Christian of just two years and "a bit of a risk". However, David expressed his desire to give me an opportunity and I will always be grateful to him for this.

Over the last eighteen years I have had the privilege of working closely with David and have come to know him better than most along the way. Without doubt, in my Christian life, he has inspired me more than anyone else. He helps me see the bigger picture in life and I have left his presence on many occasions believing that, yes, we can change the world. I have not agreed with him on every decision, but I will always honour him.

To honour is a decision not a feeling. We may not always agree or appreciate, but rather we choose to show respect.

So...

Honour your parents

Since my Dad died I have kept some photos close to me so that I can connect with the memory of him whenever I choose. They have been a point for healing and growing appreciation in me. My Mum is an incredible lady. Loving, generous, compassionate, and strong, she has brought a vast amount of good and benefit into my life. My Mum and Dad are not perfect and they have made mistakes. However, they are my parents and I find it easy to honour them.

Everyone has a different experience and relationship with their parents; we are unique. In this challenge, however, we are all the same; we must honour our parents.

Honour your leaders

In the Bible we read that one day Noah was found asleep on the floor after drinking too much. One of his sons found him naked and left him there whilst he told his brothers. His brothers refused, however, to look on their father in this moment of vulnerability, but rather walked into his tent backwards and covered his nakedness. The Lord spoke to me saying that in life I would have opportunities to expose nakedness in those close to me, because they, like me, had areas of vulnerability. The plan of God for me was to cover up their "nakedness" and speak to them in private where necessary.

Working with David I have had opportunities to dishonour him and have come to realise that David, like me, has weaknesses. Watching others in the Christian world fall out and air their difficulties in public strengthens my resolve to be a man of honour and loyalty. I will deal with things in private wherever possible.

Honour your leaders as people who will give an account for their lives.

Honour one another

Each person is worthy of being treated fairly and with honour. Yes, there are challenges and yes, we should honour one another.

How are you doing?

16

The More Thing

The evening arrived; the boys took their places. The master, in his cook's uniform, stationed himself at the copper; his pauper assistants ranged themselves behind him; the gruel was served out; and a long grace was said over the short commons. The gruel disappeared; the boys whispered at each other, and winked at Oliver; while his next neighbours nudged him. Child as he was, he was desperate with hunger, and reckless with misery. He rose from the table and advancing to the master, basin and spoon in hand, said, somewhat alarmed at his own temerity: "Please, sir, I want some more."

The master was a fat, healthy man, but he turned very pale. He gazed in stupefied astonishment on the small rebel for some seconds, and then clung for support to the copper. The assistants were paralysed with wonder; the boys with fear.

"What!" said the master at length, in a faint voice.

"Please, sir," replied Oliver, "I want some more."[1]

I became a Christian in November 1985 whilst visiting a friend at university. The next day I attended a church service and was overwhelmed and wept in the presence of God. I have found that nothing in life compares to the presence of God.

Recently a plumber visited my house and during a conversation he asked me about my employment. Following an attempt to make him guess (no one ever guesses, is this good?) he began to tell me of a visit to a Christian Union when he was fourteen. He explained, as though it had been the day before, of sensing a presence and being overwhelmed by the power of an invisible force. Twenty-eight years later, and not yet a Christian, he was recounting a moment with God that still lived with him. I told him what I now tell you – "There is more" – more of His presence, more of His love, more of His power.

I love Psalm 63 because it captures David's longing for God:

> *"O God, you are my God,*
>   *earnestly I seek you;*
> *my soul thirsts for you,*
>   *my body longs for you,*
> *in a dry and weary land*
>   *where there is no water."*

(Psalm 63:1)

I long for Him and these words help me find Him. I have included a number of quotes from the biography of Duncan Campbell, a revivalist who experienced encounters with God in the Hebrides.

O God...

A statement by the writer, not a debate.

> ...the Christians longed to see a renewed manifestation of God's power ... gradually in many hearts, concern deepened into a conviction that God's time to favour them had come. They began to pray and faith and expectation grew...[2]

You are my God...
A decision and confidence that the God of all is our God.

> ...Campbell's first contact with the men convinced him that he was in the company of those living on a high spiritual plane. As he walked down the road the next day his spirit discerned that God was at work; he realised that revival had already come; it would be his privilege to share in it.

Earnestly I seek you...
A priority expressing that above all other things, nearness to God is the greatest goal.

> A solemn hush came over the church that night and a young deacon whispered, "Mr Campbell, God is hovering over. He is going to break through. I can hear the rumblings of heaven's chariot wheels." ... the whole congregation lingered outside, reluctant to disperse; others had joined them, drawn from their homes by an irresistible power they had not experienced before.

My soul thirsts for you...
A cry that confesses a desperate need for Him.

> One evening as they were preparing to leave the church, an old man took his hat off, pointing excitedly in the direction of the congregation which had just left the service: "Mr Campbell, see what's happening! He has come! He has come!" The Spirit of God had fallen upon the people as they moved down towards the main road and in a few minutes they were so gripped with the subduing presence of God that no one could move any further.

My body longs for you...

A declaration that captures a physical longing for His presence.

> What the world needs to see is the wonder and beauty of God-possessed personalities. Women and men with the life of God pulsating within, who practice the presence of God and consequently make it easy for others to believe in God.

One day we will see Him, and He will be more wonderful than we ever imagined. Everything will have been worth it.

- Let's live for things beyond this life
- Let's invest in things that will outlast us
- Let's long for more of Him

There is more!

Notes
1. Charles Dickens, *Oliver Twist*, Penguin Books, 1994.
2. Andrew A. Woolsey, *Channel of Revival: Biography of Duncan Campbell*, Faith Mission, 1982.

17
The Why Thing

Recently a young lady was baptised in our church. This is her story:

"When I was thirteen my Mum died and two years later my Dad also died. Growing up as a firstborn, orphaned and entirely responsible for the life of my younger sister has not been easy. Having lost my parents, our money and inheritance, we were left alone and I was at the edge of reason. This resulted in drug abuse, suicide contemplation and other things I will not go into. There is an expression that means to lose all you have: to hit rock bottom. I hit rock bottom and I realised that when you hit rock bottom there is a rock at the bottom. His name is Jesus.

From the pit of nothingness, God has blessed me in my life, rescued me and provided me with everything I lacked. I now have a job, wonderful friends in my cell group and a chance to go to school. I have found Him to be my Father, Mentor, Saviour, my courage, my wisdom, my resting place, my daily bread and my strength."

She has found in the midst of huge challenges that Jesus is faithful. However, the "why?" question remains.

Susan's brother was severely autistic and her teenage years had their challenges. Iain didn't speak and had behaviour patterns that were at times distressing to others. He was loved and cared for in a family that accepted him and got on with life, even with its intense difficulties. An article written about Iain records the following: "At fourteen his mind still has the unreasoning incomprehension of a toddler. He needs constant care to protect him from himself. The head banging goes on. With no sense of danger he would hurl himself at moving wheels if his parents were not alert and protective. Iain struggles to go to sleep and his parents often sit with him for hours before he drops off..." I never had the joy of meeting Iain as he died of a mystery virus at the same time Susan and I began to date. I am proud, though, of the sacrifice that Ray and Margaret, Janet and Susan, gave so that Iain could be as happy as possible.

Having talked to the parents of a number of autistic children, I am left with more questions than answers. So many of them face private battles and traumas from a condition that is now widely known, but not widely understood. The "why" question remains.

Why do joy and sadness, laughter and tears, questions and answers, exist at the same time?

Why are there so many things we can't understand?

Over the years, trying to support those who have lost a loved one because of suicide, standing with couples who have experienced miscarriages or barrenness and trying to understand long-term sickness and trauma, I have been left with many unanswered questions.

In life we all face the reality of suffering, but we can also have comfort.

Suffering happens to everyone

All of us at some time face pain and sadness.

Suffering does not mean God loves us more or less

We are loved and there is nothing we can do to make God love us more. Suffering is never a sign that we are unloved. Suffering should make us more like Jesus and it may lead to maturity and fruitfulness, but it doesn't make Jesus love us more.

Suffering will lead to comfort

We may not understand or have all our questions answered, but the promise of the Bible is that comfort will be given to us (2 Corinthians 1:3–4).

Comfort comes from God

He is the source of all comfort and in our brokenness we can know that He stands with us.

Comfort is to be passed onto others

With the comfort we have received the Bible compels us to stand with others and bring them hope and love. We can love and we can point people to Jesus.

Max Lucado writes,

> And when you see Him, you'll set your luggage down. Just as a returning soldier drops his duffel bag when he sees his wife, you'll drop everything when you see your father. Those you love will applaud. But all the noise will cease when He cups your chin and says, "Welcome home." And with scarred hand He'll wipe every tear from your eye. And you will dwell in the house of the Lord forever.[1]

There will be no more tears and questions in heaven.

Note
1. Max Lucado, *Travelling Light*, Thomas Nelson, 2006.

18

The Loyalty Thing

I met Susan in a primary school classroom in November 1985. She worked with my Mum and had written to me after hearing I had become a Christian the previous weekend. The letter had intrigued me as it contained Bible verses and was written in a style I was not familiar with. Later when I walked into Susan's classroom, I believe I fell in love with her from the first moment I saw her. She had a beauty that was both on the surface and deep within her as a person. Her commitment to Jesus was compelling for me.

We are now in our nineteenth year of marriage and Susan is the most important person in my life. She is my best friend, closest confidante and biggest supporter. We are "doing life" together and every day I would choose her all over again. When I made staggeringly challenging promises to Susan at our marriage, I was placing a sign around my neck that says, "no longer available". At times we have disagreed and at times she says I am not easy to live with (surely not!), but we have decided that, with God's help, we will always be loyal to one another, whatever the cost.

So what is loyalty?

- Loyalty is to show unswerving support or enduring and committed allegiance
- Loyalty comes out of relationship, not requirement

- Loyalty is a choice, not a feeling
- Loyalty is spoken of in a moment, but proven over time

God's loyalty to us is absolute, so where can we show loyalty?

Loyalty in our relationship with Jesus

Are you on strong ground? Do you love Jesus and are you committed to never giving up? If I was in the student bedroom where I became a Christian in November 1985, I would write on a bit of paper, *"David, the choice you are about to make is the best decision you will ever make and it will open doors you have never dreamt about. It is the reason for your existence."*

Loyalty in our marriages

I saw it quoted recently that people are more likely to change their marriage partners than their football club. 70% of people feel that cheating and disloyalty are more "socially acceptable" nowadays than they used to be. When I held Susan's hand and said, "To love and cherish till death us do part" that was it, forever.

Loyalty in our friendships

Human relationships depend on loyalty. In fact, without it, the fabric of our society loses its stability. Disloyalty and betrayal are devastating.

Loyalty in our churches

Give financially, serve and invest your time, pray for your leaders and live as an example to others. If everyone in your church was like you, what would your church be like?

Loyalty in our responsibilities

Be a brilliant employee, serve in your home, maintain your role in the church and be loyal.

To me, loyalty is one of the greatest characteristics in a person and I look for it in people. I have not faced much betrayal, so my views are not based on fear, I simply believe loyalty is a Jesus thing.

The Men Thing

Women are compassionate, loving and caring and they cry when they are happy
Women have the ability to keep smiling even if exhausted
Women will stop at nothing to get what they think is best for their children
Women can turn a simple meal into an occasion and know how to make a man feel like a king
Women know how to comfort a sick friend and will go the extra mile
Women know how to entertain children for hours on end
Women have a will of iron under that soft exterior
Women are easily brought to tears by injustice
Women make the world a much happier place to live in

Men can move heavy things and deal with spiders.[1]

Men are all different, with unique personalities and characters that can't be generalised or boxed. However, we face battles that can leave us all feeling undermined, restricted and powerless.

In the New Testament Paul talks about the kind of men who receive recognition from God – men on their guard, firm in their faith, full of courage, who act and live in love; men devoted to serve, who know how to submit and supply what others lack.

So here are my ten thoughts for men:

Walk with Jesus

He is the ultimate role model – the greatest man ever to live and we need Him. Read your Bible, pray every day, go to church and get involved, commit your life to Him and be teachable and vulnerable.

Be accountable

Who really knows you? Who checks up on you? Who says "no" to you? Have someone who regularly asks you the hard questions, cuts through the rubbish, is not easily fooled and is committed to you.

Deal with your eyes

If you watch men and how they look at women you will soon want to be different. Set new standards for yourself, focus on the eyes of a person and deal with your "eye gate".

Conquer pornography

Whether it's in a magazine, on television, or the Internet, don't kid yourself, you are responsible for what you look at.

- Sign up, at www.covenanteyes.com and the sites you visit will be emailed weekly to a friend
- Never turn the television on without checking the schedule pages first
- Get rid of satellite television if you can't control yourself

Be generous

Never be tight with friends and loved ones. Be the first to give. Look for ways to show generosity without anyone knowing it was you and always sow in abundance to God.

Be chivalrous

Even if they refuse it or never say "thank you", always hold open a door for a lady, give up your seat for them when the occasion arises and look for ways to be kind. Be the first to be thankful and live with a sense of gratitude for what you have, not focusing on what you don't have.

Be disciplined

Don't be mastered by anything other than the purpose of God. Exercise self-control with food, alcohol, taking exercise and sensible bedtimes.

Have fun and laugh a lot

I recently spent a week with a new friend and laughed more than I have done for a long time. I returned refreshed, strengthened and life was more in perspective.

Be ordered

Don't live a chaotic life, but allow order and structure to surround you – it doesn't prevent you from being spontaneous. Make a will and leave your finances ordered, so if you die, this isn't an area that your wife has to worry about. I organise all the finances in our home and I have created a file so that if I die, everything is clear for Susan and she will know what to do. This isn't morbid, but responsible.

Don't underestimate who you are

You are a man of God, armed with strength, given a shield of victory, sustained by God who, "stoops down to make you great" (see Psalm 18:35). Your best years are ahead of you, the power of God Almighty is in you and nothing can stop you being all you are called to be except you.

The poet Josiah Gilbert Holland wrote,

> God, give us men! A time like this demands
> Strong minds, great hearts, true faith and ready hands;
> Men whom the lust of office does not kill;
> Men whom the spoils of office can not buy;
> Men who possess opinions and a will;
> Men who have honour; men who will not lie ...

Note
1. J. John and Mark Stibbe, *A Barrel of Fun*, Monarch, 2003.

20

The Worship Thing

Jesus had been invited for a meal and He was regarded as the guest of honour. Certain rules of etiquette, therefore, would be expected.

- The customary greeting was a kiss. This was not an expression of affection, rather a polite acknowledgment of the guest's arrival. To ignore this was equal to ignoring the person and was seen as an insult.
- The washing of feet was also mandatory before a meal. If the guest was honoured the host would perform the task himself.
- Finally, a thoughtful host would offer olive oil as a refreshing deodorant for the guest.

At the home of Simon, even though Jesus was an honoured guest, He was given no kiss, no water for His feet and no oil for His head.

A certain immoral woman heard that Jesus was there and she brought a beautiful jar filled with expensive perfume. She came into the room and knelt at Jesus' feet and wept. Her tears fell on His feet and she kissed His feet and poured perfume on them. Then she dried His feet with her hair.

The woman was once someone's little baby – the object of a mother's hopes and dreams. Maybe her husband had deserted her; maybe her heart had hardened; but one thing is certain: this woman knew what it was to be despised and unwelcome. No decent person would speak to her, welcome her, or acknowledge her. Perhaps she had listened to Jesus speak; perhaps she had begun to sense the love of God for her.

She sees Jesus being dishonoured and she walks into the room and kneels at His feet. She begins to weep tears of sadness for what she has done and tears of gratitude that Jesus doesn't send her away. She lets her hair down and wipes His feet – a humiliating act of self-abasement. Finally she brings the best she can and pours ointment on His feet.

Jesus said,

> "She kissed my feet to bring a greeting; she washed and dried my feet with her tears and her hair; and she anointed my feet with oil. I tell you, her sins – and they are many – have been forgiven. Therefore she has shown me much love."
>
> (Paraphrase of Luke 7:44–47)

So, this worship thing...

We could talk about songs and music, instruments and structure. We could reflect on lyrics, liturgy, style and opinion, but more important than all of the above, let's simply do this:

- Let's kneel at His feet.
- Let's weep tears of gratitude.
- Let's wash His feet with our praise.
- Let's anoint Him by an offering of our best.

Jesus is Lord. He is all and He is everything!

21

The Burden Thing

I had the privilege of listening to Mark Buntain speak shortly before he died. He pioneered a phenomenal work with the poor in India and carried an immense burden for them. He was known as a humble man who served others.

> "On one of his trips to the United States he was invited to the home of a pastor. After dinner they retired to the living room where the pastor had thoughtfully obtained a collection of Indian music. One of the tracks was the haunting 'Song of India'. Mark was captivated and asked for the track again and again. After a couple of hours of this monotony the family excused themselves and went to bed.
>
> Around two in the morning the pastor awoke and could still hear the music. He crept downstairs and saw Mark lying on the floor. Tears washed down his cheeks. Hoarse from hours of praying he was still whispering, 'India, my India – Jesus, please save India.'"[1]

To carry a burden is a responsibility and needs to be prayed through. We all carry different burdens. Here are a few of mine...

- For all the children who are abused, afraid and vulnerable in our country.
  Lord, in your mercy hear my prayer

- For the 170,000 babies that will be aborted in the next twelve months.
  Lord, in your mercy hear my prayer
- For those who can't face life and mistakenly see suicide as the answer to set them free.
  Lord, in your mercy hear my prayer
- For women who sell their bodies and for the men who use them.
  Lord, in your mercy hear my prayer
- For women who are beaten in their own homes and lack the love they long for.
  Lord, in your mercy hear my prayer
- For Christians who long to be married and find themselves waiting.
  Lord, in your mercy hear my prayer
- For the nine million senior people in our nation.
  Lord, in your mercy hear my prayer
- For the hundreds of thousands of people who are imprisoned for believing in Jesus.
  Lord, in your mercy hear my prayer
- For parents who grieve the death of their children.
  Lord, in your mercy hear my prayer
- For all the people who struggle with depression.
  Lord, in your mercy hear my prayer
- For those who battle with cancer and long-term sickness.
  Lord, in your mercy hear my prayer
- For the millions of people who live without Jesus and miss the very reason for their existence.
  Lord, in your mercy hear my prayer

What's your burden?

Take some time to pray

Note
1. Douglas Wead, *The Compassionate Touch*, Bethany House, 1980.

22

The Teenagers Thing

I recently sat with a group of sixty teenagers for a question time. The questions they asked included, "What is your greatest regret? How much are you paid? Do you find some preaching boring? How far can we go in a relationship?" At the end I was given a few moments to say anything else I wanted to pass on. Sixty lives, listening, open, ready to hear – now that's a responsibility.

Here's what I would like to say to every teenager:

God thinks you are precious

You weren't a mistake, a result of failed contraception, or a little surprise. You weren't born by chance – the result of a biological reaction – you were created and planned by God, who loves you passionately and longs to be close to you.

Your parents make mistakes

There are no perfect parents. You may be in a great family in which love is shown and you feel secure. Even you, listen! Your parents are not perfect. Forgive them for their mistakes. Forgive and learn from them so you can be even better when you become a parent.

Be yourself

There's only one of you and you don't have to be like everyone else. Peer pressure is a challenge and to be accepted is important, but you are unique, so be you.

Preserve your virginity

If you are still a virgin at seventeen are you all right? YES! Don't compromise a gift for a moment's enjoyment. Don't give this part of yourself to anyone until they have shown you commitment in marriage first. You can lose your virginity quite easily, but you can never regain it.

Don't worry about masturbation

I believe God's ideal is for you to live without masturbation, but if it is occasional it isn't a major issue. Can God still love me? Yes. Will I go blind? No. Am I the only person to be tempted? No. Be careful what you watch and think about, stay healthy, and ask God to help you cope with your sexual drive. Don't worry.

You don't have to...

...get drunk, take drugs, sniff glue, watch pornography, love football, watch 18-rated films, swear, be difficult at home, have a strop, harm yourself, belittle who you are, have every trendy label, go to nightclubs, have money, have a boyfriend/girlfriend, get an A* in every exam, or be perfect. Really, you don't have to!

Dream big

What a life you have ahead of you, full of incredible possibilities and massive potential. Dream of changing the world and then go and do it. Let no one tell you it can't be done.

Love Jesus

At the age of twelve His parents found Jesus in church, talking to the leaders and asking them questions. They were amazed at His understanding and His answers. Jesus is the ultimate hero. He didn't have the money of Bill Gates, the football skills of Wayne Rooney, or the record sales of Robbie Williams, but His birth date set the timeline for the world, His life is talked about more than any other and His death changed history. Jesus is alive and to know Him is the greatest thing in life.

Go for it, you are amazing!

23

The Remember Thing

When was the last time you simply lost yourself in Jesus? Maybe, for a moment, His grace and love and the hope for your future overwhelmed you. Perhaps you knelt down or jumped around the room, or quietly stood and met with Jesus.

There have been times when I have stopped and realised that Jesus truly is the centre of my life. In these moments I can't imagine what I would do without Him. He is beyond explanation and I need Him more than breath.

The following is a story from *The Signature of Jesus* by Brennan Manning:

> One summer in Iowa City, Iowa, I directed a five-day retreat for a little group of Christians. The small number allowed for an unusual degree of dialogue, sharing, and communion.
>
> One mid-thirtyish woman in the group was conspicuous by her silence. She was a slender, attractive nun, who neither responded, nor communicated with any of us.
>
> On the afternoon of the fourth day I invited each person to share what God had been doing in his or her life the past few days. After a couple of minute's silence, the nun, whom I shall call Christine, reached for her journal and said, "Something happened to me yesterday, and I wrote it down. You were speaking on the compassion of Jesus. At the end of your talk,

you prayed that we might experience what you had just shared. You asked us to close our eyes. Almost the moment I did, something happened. In faith I was transported into a large ballroom filled with people. I was sitting by myself on a wooden chair, when a man approached me, took my hand, and led me onto the floor. He held me in his arms and led me in the dance.

The tempo of the music increased and we whirled faster and faster. The man's eyes never left my face. His radiant smile covered me with warmth, delight, and a sense of acceptance. Everyone else stopped dancing. They were staring at us. The beat of the music increased as we pirouetted around the room in reckless rhythm. I glanced at his hands, and then I knew. Brilliant wounds of a battle long ago, almost like a signature carved in flesh. The music tapered to a slow, lilting melody, and Jesus rocked me back and forth. As the dance ended, He pulled me close to Him. 'Do you know what He whispered?' "

At this moment everyone in the chapel strained forward. Tears rolled down Christine's cheeks. A full minute of silence ensued. Her face was beaming and when she spoke, she said, "Jesus whispered to me, 'Christine, I'm wild about you.' "[1]

- In the busyness of life, take time to be with Him.
- In the pressure of schedules, don't miss Him.
- In the desire for efficiency, don't forget Him.
- In the familiarity of faith, don't take Him for granted.

We need many things in life and above all of these we need Jesus. To touch Him and sense His presence sweeping over us is incomparable.

He is wild about you.

Note
1. Brennan Manning, *The Signature of Jesus: On the Pages of Our Lives*, Multnomah, 1992.

24

The Marriage Thing

Susan wrote this poem for me shortly after we were married:

> And after the moonlight has faded
> Kind, mellow, flattering light
> Where shadows blend with muted tones
> And after the roses have at last withered
> Fallen petals scattered on the winds of time
>
> In the brightest of sunlight
> Where shadows are seen for what they are
> And reality cannot hide
> Where blemishes and wounds are glaringly visible
> And we are discovered
> Then will you still say "I love you"?
>
> Now we have the privilege
> To love as our creator does
> To see what no one else sees
> And still remain faithful
> And still keep the promises of long ago
> And still say in truth, "I love you"
>
> A love, always deep, is now so much more
> Now it is wide and long and high, as well as deep

For it embraces not just the you I thought you were
But now the you I find you are
The height and depth and breadth
The wonder and the mystery
The known and yet to be known of you

As we go on our journey together
May each, "I love you", however often said
Be more special and more truthful than the last

Susan Hind

So, marriage – a few thoughts...

Communicate

Men and women are different, so learn to communicate with each other. Plan times to both listen and talk together and make sure you have heard what the other person has said. This takes time and is always worth it.

Be accountable

Susan and I love and trust one another and I have also asked her to regularly ask me the following questions:

- Have you read anything you regret?
- Have you watched anything you shouldn't have?
- Have you been careful with your words?
- Is there another woman you have been thinking about?
- Have you been greedy?
- Have you been wasteful with money?
- Have you any unforgiveness in your heart?
- Are you anxious or restless about anything?

Talk to one another and don't have secrets. In the light, darkness is banished.

Plan romance

Whether it is a meal out, a walk in the country, or a cuddle, not all romance can be spontaneous. Even intimacy together can be planned. A friend of mine once said, "It's difficult for my wife and I to relax in the bedroom if there are three children at the door asking why it's locked and what are we doing in there."

Forgive quickly

I'm told that some couples never have disagreements. I belong to the majority who do. Making up can be fun and working through challenges strengthens the foundations of a relationship. Sort out your differences and don't go to sleep still angry.

Get help if you need it

There are many people who take marriage counselling, so don't be proud if help will help.

Enjoy the journey

It may have a few moments of challenge, but marriage is wonderful.

You can have a fantastic marriage.

25
The Lost Thing

A young girl grows up on a cherry orchard in Michigan. Her parents, a bit old fashioned, tend to overreact to her and after a heated argument she runs away.

Deciding to hide in Detroit, after a few days she is drawn into a lifestyle that leads to drug addiction and prostitution. Before long she becomes ill and homeless. One night as she lies awake, listening for footsteps, everything about her life looks different. She no longer feels like a woman of the world. She feels like a little girl, lost in a cold and frightening city. Her pockets are empty and she's hungry, she needs a fix, she's desperate, then, in a moment, she remembers home.

She finds a phone and when the answering machine kicks in she says, "Dad, Mum, it's me. I was wondering about maybe coming home. I'm catching a bus up your way and I'll get there around midnight tomorrow. If you want to come, I'll be there for a few moments."

It takes about seven hours for a bus to make all the stops between Detroit and Traverse City, and she thinks of all the flaws in her plan. What if they didn't get the message, what if they have forgotten about her. All the time she prepares her speech, "Dad, I'm sorry. I know I was wrong. Can you forgive me?"

When the bus rolls into the station she pauses and then steps off the bus. Not one of the scenes that have played out in her mind prepares her for what she sees. There, with her Mum and Dad, stands a group of forty brothers, sisters, aunts, uncles, and a grandmother. They are all cheering and wearing party hats and taped across the entire wall is a banner that reads "Welcome Home".[1]

At nineteen I had heard about God and I believed in God, but I was lost. An American missionary, Doug, having shared the message of Jesus with me, looked at me and said, "So that's Christianity, David. You can go away and think about it, or we can pray now, it's up to you." In that moment I needed to respond and discover the reason I was alive.

I never realised that one prayer could have so much impact. Twenty-one years later I believe that the question I was asked on that day was the most important of my life and my prayer the most important I will ever say. I was lost and then I was found.

We can learn a lot about God's heart for lost people in the Book of Jonah.

God is always thinking about lost people (Jonah 1:1–2)

A lost person lives without Christ in their lives and they are His highest priority. He wants no one to be lost and everyone to be found.

God will move heaven and earth for lost people (Jonah 1:4)

He has done, and will do, everything He can to find us. There could be no higher cost than the cross.

God will always hear the prayer that leads to lost people finding Him (Jonah 2:1–9)

We can communicate with God about anything, but when we talk to Him about the lost we touch His heart.

God gives second chances so lost people can be found (Jonah 3:1–2)

All of us can get up, start again, and begin to reach lost people.

God is able to reach every lost person – we only have to do our part (Jonah 3:10)

Jonah did his part and God did His and 120,000 people responded. God has no limits and anything can happen.

We all have our part to play and we all have people to reach.

Lost people matter to God.

Note
1. Phillip Yancey, *What's So Amazing About Grace?*, Zondervan, 2002.

26

The Serving Thing

The Top Ten of Everything[1] was a Christmas present in our house this year. Did you know that Japan eats more eggs, China has more sheep, India has more cinema attendees and the UK consumes more breakfast cereal, than any other country? Did you know that six of the world's top ten bestselling newspapers are Japanese, 5.5 trillion cigarettes a year are smoked and Christianity has, at 2.159 billion, the most followers?

If God were to draw up a list of the greatest human attributes what would be in His top ten? I think faithfulness, loyalty and love would be there. I also believe that a serving heart would be near the top.

Jesus turned the idea of serving on its head.

- His mission was to serve.
- His desire was to serve.
- His reactions were to serve.
- He was a servant and He came to give.

In our society, self-importance, rights and selfishness are often the driving forces. How should we respond? How should we order our time so we can serve?

Make time to serve Jesus

The One who washes our feet and lays down His life is worthy of our love and gratitude. I must take time to worship Him and let Him love me.

Make time to serve your family and friends

Husbands, wives, parents, children, and friends, are given to us to serve.

Make time to serve at work

Whether in the home or as an employee we should serve and be grateful. If I reach the position when I believe certain tasks are below me, I should step back from ministry, because Jesus set a different standard.

Make time to serve in your church

Turning up early on a Sunday morning to a city centre church, one can often see the evidence of a lively Saturday night out in Nottingham. I remember seeing one of our female stewards cleaning up human excrement outside our church before anyone else arrived. I realised that nothing I said that day on the platform would speak louder for Jesus than this act of service.

Make time to serve in your community

Rubbish on the streets, litter thrown out of car windows, old people standing up on buses whilst younger people fill the seats ... we need to be different. There are always people we can help – a senior person to visit, local issues to support and Christianity to work out.

Serving is natural to some and caught by others, however, it is not an option.

Serving demonstrates our faith and is a life call.

To serve is to be like Jesus.

Note
1. Russell Ash, *The Top Ten of Everything 2006*, DK Publishing, 2005.

27

The Musicians Thing

Born into a musical family I had the privilege of being taught instruments as a child and was given the opportunity to sing as a chorister. At eleven I sang the first verse of "Once in Royal David's City" at the Christmas Eve recital in Southwell Minster, which was an honour. Leaving the choir at thirteen I was part of a rock band called "Anaconda" for three or four years. Since becoming a Christian I have had the opportunity to record albums and sing in gatherings of hundreds and occasionally thousands.

I will always be grateful that my parents instilled in me a love for music and the importance of learning an instrument. We have passed this on to our children. Thomas has passed his grade eight saxophone and piano, whilst Samuel has an eclectic taste and a fantastic ear for music.

When Tom was twelve he came back from being involved in a music group with children and was despondent. He had been asked to lead and felt it hadn't gone very well. He didn't have long to prepare, his keyboard wasn't very good and he couldn't hear himself. Not only that, but the PA wasn't working properly, the preacher spoke for too long and the band didn't have enough time. Finally, he was desperate for the loo and couldn't sing very well.

I talked to him about practising hard, being humble, dealing with ego, God's tests and what to do when it goes wrong. In the future, when he stands on bigger stages than I have, I pray he will remember.

Inside the church, music plays a big part in worship, atmosphere and as a tool for leading people into the presence of God. Musicians therefore, have a responsibility to prepare themselves before God.

Here are a few of my thoughts for musicians and worship leaders:

Be grateful for the gift of music

How did God create music? There are relatively few notes and yet we will never come to the end of the amazing variety of sound that can be created using them. Don't presume, be grateful, and play for the One who had the idea of music.

Develop your gift

Whilst recording *Painting a Picture*, my latest album, Ben Castle came to record some saxophone. I was completely inspired by one of the best saxophonists in our country. After he had played we talked about the hours he aims to practise every day as time allows. We are not all able to do this (grateful parents of children learning the violin, note!), however, don't be lazy.

Deal with your ego

Music is powerful and can shape our world. I recently stood at a U2 concert with around 70,000 others and saw the power of influence through music. There are moments in worship when there is great power. In these moments Jesus is the focus – it is all for Him and we are simply vessels. A record producer talked to me about the difference between high and low maintenance musicians. The high maintenance ones need constant encouragement, special treatment and appreciation. Grow up and be low maintenance.

Develop consistency in character

Arrive on time, tune your instrument, be reliable and don't be on an emotional rollercoaster. How easily are you offended? Is Jesus more important to you than the music?

Practise the presence of God

Learn to allow the presence of God to flow through your music. At times, less is more, and to be sensitive to Him can change any atmosphere.

Keep worshipping.

28
The No Sex Before Marriage Thing

There is no easy way to write this chapter; no easy way to be funny; no easy way to say what is a deep conviction for me, so here we go...

I believe sex is great. God is pro-sex and sex is His gift. He created men and women with separate sexual identities, not for separateness, but for oneness. I believe that sex is for marriage only and that to reserve our virginity for marriage is always the best option.

In western society particularly, we are bombarded from every angle with the message that it is normal and even "right" for us to have sex with whoever we like, whenever we like. This is wrong.

I have a number of questions about life that I would love to have answered. One is why God did not make sexual desire a gift one receives after marriage. You can imagine the scene: "I now pronounce you husband and wife – you may kiss the bride." They look at one another in a way they never have before and say, "Yippee! Let's leave the party, now!" But it doesn't work like that. That's why sex is one of the biggest issues for the majority of the population.

Why not intercourse before marriage?

Sex is a spiritual act as well as a physical one. Jesus said a man will leave his father and mother and be united with his wife and they will become "one flesh". When we have intercourse with another person, we become one flesh with them. When that happens outside of the covenant of marriage, a bond is forged between two people that creates an ungodly tie.

The Bible forbids adultery and casual sex. Adultery is sexual intercourse between a married person and someone to whom they are not married (Matthew 19:18). Casual sex, or fornication, is intercourse between two unmarried people (1 Corinthians 6:13; 1 Thessalonians 4:3).

Sex is intended to be a demonstration of love within a committed relationship. God's plan is for this always to be in the context of marriage. He does not want you to feel abandoned and rejected when someone takes your virginity and then leaves you. How many times have we heard people comment,

- But it's so difficult and we know we are going to get married.
- As long as we don't have full intercourse, surely it's OK?
- But it's only a little bit of harmless fun!
- How do you expect me to wait?

Where do we draw the line?

I believe the following guidelines are wise: outside of marriage we can hold hands, we can embrace and we can kiss and that's it! This may not be popular, but it's right, and we mustn't sin against grace by imagining we can do what we like and it has no consequences. To keep within these parameters will help us.

How can I survive?

If you live in obedience you will know the presence of God and He will not allow you to be tempted beyond that which you can bear. He always gives a way out (1 Corinthians 10:13).

Your virginity is precious and a gift to the person you will marry. If you have made mistakes, then Jesus offers you a fresh start.

29

The Words Thing

I heard about a minister who tripped over his words as he was introducing a time for his congregation to greet one another in church. He meant to say, "Let's feel free to greet one another." However, he actually said, "Let's have a free feel with one another"! In public speaking there is no easy recovery from a comment like this. I was praying with a colleague for one of our single missionaries recently and I don't know why I said it – I meant to say, "great success" – but I prayed out loud that she would have "a year of great sex"!

Words have incredible power.

They can make you laugh

After the above prayer we all stopped and laughed and everyone enjoyed my acute embarrassment and feeble attempts to give an explanation.

They can make you cry

When Susan's brother died, a few days later Margaret, her Mum, had a dream in which Iain spoke to her and said, "I'm alright, Mum." He had not spoken for many years.

They can leave you inspired

Churchill on 4th June 1940, spoke to the country and said,

> "We shall fight with growing confidence and growing strength in the air. We shall defend our Island, whatever the cost may be. We shall fight on the beaches, we shall fight on the landing grounds, we shall fight in the fields and in the streets, we shall fight in the hills. We shall never surrender..."

They can reassure you

Maybe you can remember times when you were young and a parent said to you, "Don't worry, everything is alright." As a child I fell off the edge of the bath and severely bit my tongue. In the hospital I wouldn't open my mouth and was eventually persuaded to do so by the reassuring sight of my Mum sticking her own tongue out at me and saying my name.

They can hurt you

To be told we are clumsy, unplanned or not wanted, can leave deep scars in our lives.

They can heal you

The Bible says you are a wonderful person, loved, special and precious. Whatever others have said to you, this is the real truth.

To tame our tongues is a day-by-day challenge.

To build up and inspire, rather than to bring down and damage, is a minute-by-minute journey.

The psalmist puts it like this:

> *"May the words of my mouth and the meditation of my heart*
> *be pleasing in your sight,*
> *O LORD..."*

(Psalm 19:14)

Jesus' words are the greatest words ever spoken. They are real, colourful, ethical and life changing. As we follow His words, our words will change.

Enough said.

30
The Parenting Thing

It's Saturday night and Susan, Sam, Tom and I are in the middle of a "Time for TATT" (talking at the table). The idea is that each person in turn gets to talk about their week, their concerns and areas for reflection with the family. Everyone else has to listen and can only speak if invited to by the person whose turn it is. In its ideal form it is the best way I have seen to communicate and give room for honesty and vulnerability in a family. Even very recently, when his younger brother was away at a youth weekend, Samuel, at seventeen, came for his customary Saturday night chat, ready to share several moving and well thought out comments about his life. We have had some fantastic times and others when I was glad that only God sees everything!

Being a parent is one of the greatest privileges and responsibilities given to people. To be trusted with the life of another is awesome. To then be asked to train and inspire them to stand on our shoulders and reach their full potential is a "gulp" moment.

Happy memories are mixed in with moments of vulnerability. From the moment they are born to their teenage years and beyond we ask ourselves many questions about our children, including the following:

- Are they feeding OK?
- Is it right that they are not speaking yet?

- What school should they go to?
- How much television should they watch?
- How can we help them make more friends?
- What *are* they saying for so long on the phone?
- Where are they at 11.30pm?
- Will they be safe?

I believe God's original plan was for a husband and wife, together, to bring up their children. Today, for many families and for many reasons, parenting alone is a reality. With God's help, though, I believe all of us can succeed in our parenting.

A few principles Susan and I are aiming to live out:

Accept the strengths and weaknesses of your own upbringing

Some of us had desperate childhoods and others were over protected. Some could never talk about or express their emotions and others had a listening ear. Some had no visible Mum, Dad or permanent home, others never knew love. Some lived through divorce, affairs, or grew up in care homes, separated from brothers and sisters. Some have only positive memories and some have only negative ones.

Don't live in limitation. Don't try to over compensate. Forgive and move on.

Be teachable and find role models

Before the release of my last album I paid for a singing lesson with a lady who could help me with my breathing. She knew more than I did and was able to show me a different technique and it really helped. There are many parents who have already walked the path you are walking. Look for ones you respect, ask them to help you and be open to their advice.

Learn to listen

Listening builds a bridge over which communication can pass for a lifetime. The more a child becomes aware of a parent's willingness to listen, the more a parent will hear.

Talk carefully

Be careful how you speak about your children. Always be honest, encouraging and consistent. Explain to them why you say "no" sometimes, keep your promises and release the power of "sorry" and "I forgive you" in your family.

Give them boundaries

Every child, young person and adult, needs boundaries.

Create memories

Fulfilled lives are built on rich memories. Decide to do something memorable with your children today.

You can be a fantastic parent.

31

The First Steps Thing

During a time of worship at the Christian Centre some years ago, we were singing a song about how Jesus is precious. During this song, Jean, a good friend of mine, felt God say to her, "That's how I feel about you."

Some time later she was talking to another person and said, "It seems easier to hear God speak about the little things, but harder to hear Him on the bigger things in life."

That night God spoke to her again and said, "Your priorities are wrong. I did firstly speak to you about the biggest thing and that is, 'you are precious to me'."

To be forgiven by His grace and know we are precious to Him are two of the first steps in our walk with Jesus. Alongside these there are a number of other "first steps" that we can take.

In Acts chapter 9, Paul the apostle, after he begins to believe in Jesus, sets an example that all new believers would do well to follow:

- He is humbled (v. 6)
- He receives a miracle (v. 18)
- He is baptised in the Spirit (v. 17)
- He is baptised in water (v. 18)

- He takes on food and becomes stronger (v. 19)
- He shares his faith (v. 20)
- He joins a church (v. 26)

I believe these first steps are still vital today.

Humble yourself

Humility is something we choose in life. The Bible says, *"What does the LORD require of you? To act justly and to love mercy and to walk humbly with your God"* (Micah 6:8). If we make a start, God will help us on the journey of humility.

Anticipate miracles

Never underestimate the power of a changed life. God is still able and nothing is too hard for Him. Expect and believe for miracles in your life.

Be baptised in the Spirit

To know the power of the Holy Spirit in our lives propels us into a more intimate walk with Jesus. It's not complicated. Jesus says that if we ask, we will receive (John 16:24).

Be baptised in water

I was baptised as a baby, confirmed in Southwell Minster and then became a Christian. To be baptised as a Christian was then a simple act of obedience in following Jesus' example.

Eat and become stronger

Begin to read the Bible and you will learn to hear God speak to you. Pray that the words will come alive.

Share your faith

To tell another what Jesus has done for you does not just impact them. It is a step that leads you into a deeper knowledge of Him (see Philemon 1:6).

Join a church

We all need people and Christianity is a personal faith to be celebrated with others.

How are you doing with the first steps?

32

The Smell Thing

In 2005 we travelled to Spain on a family holiday. I was pleased with myself for the "amazing deal" I had been able to secure for a hire car – a moment of male efficiency and success. However, when we drove away from the airport we were in the smallest car I have ever been in. Samuel is 6ft 2ins and Tom on the way to 6ft. The moment I saw them scrunched up in the back seat with a case and bags on their knees that wouldn't fit in the boot (which was more like a glove box), was the moment I realised this could be a very expensive "cheap deal".

When the car broke down for the second time, it was the moment of realisation for me that I had been ripped off. We called the garage out and after a long wait and ruined plans we were asked to drive the car back to the airport to change vehicles. I was told that they knew about my situation and that I was a priority case to quickly receive a bigger car. Susan and I drove the distance and arrived at the hire desk ready to forgive and put the whole thing behind us. When a sign declaring "everyone at lunch" greeted us, I had a moment when I wasn't very much like Jesus. I marched into the café and demanded that one of the staff who were eating come and serve me.

A lively discussion ensued during which the staff member swore at me three times (I remember because I asked him to repeat the word he used). Later when I drove away, Susan quietly listened as I complained of the poor service, the unacceptable comments, the fact that I deserved better and that I intended to complain. When we arrived at our apartment I carried on reading *The Ragamuffin Gospel* by Brennan Manning and came to a part where he writes,

> Ragamuffins don't sit down to be served, they kneel down to serve. When there is food on their plate, they don't whine about the monotonous menu or the cracked plate. Glad for a full stomach, they give thanks for the smallest gift. They do not grow impatient and irritable with the dismal service in department stores, because they so often fail to be good servants themselves.[1]

I found a bad smell on me and I knew I was wrong. I repented and asked God to change my heart. When we returned the car I apologised to the assistant who had sworn at me and gave him some money to buy a lunch that wouldn't be disturbed. He also apologised and we shook hands.

So the smell thing...

Your spiritual smell is vital

A monk once said, "When I leave a conversation with someone, I ask myself the questions, 'Did they find Christ in me?'; 'Did I find Christ in them?'"

As a Christian my rights are less important than the will of God. So many times I have said things I shouldn't have. I have reacted in a way that wasn't Christlike and I have been selfish. And yet I want to be the fragrance of Christ and I want to be more like Him.

How are you doing on this score? Here's a test:

- Do I make people feel special?
- Do I leave people feeling more, or less encouraged?

- Are people more or less focused on Jesus when they have been with me?
- Am I self-centred or others-centred?
- Do I talk about myself or focus on others?
- Do I expect a certain standard of food, accommodation, style or treatment?
- Am I really content whatever I face?
- Is the Jesus smell around me?

No matter who you are – however ordinary, however important, however wealthy and famous – your spiritual smell is vital.

How are you doing?

Note

1. Brennan Manning, *The Ragamuffin Gospel*, Multnomah Publishers, 2000.

33
The Giants Thing

Jim Elliot was a man committed to doing the will of God. In the autumn of 1955, missionary pilot Nate Saint spotted an Auca village and during the months that followed, Jim and several fellow missionaries, dropped gifts from a plane, attempting to befriend the hostile tribe.

In January of 1956, he and four companions landed on a beach of the Curaray River in eastern Ecuador. They had several friendly contacts with the tribe but two days later, on 8th January, all five men were speared and hacked to death. Jim Elliot was twenty-eight.

Some years later his wife Elizabeth Elliot bravely returned to share the Christian message with those who killed her husband and many Aucas came to accept Christ as Saviour. She then wrote a number of books that have been the catalyst for sending thousands into the mission fields.

Elizabeth overcame the giants of fear, intimidation, unforgiveness and bitterness that could have prevented her living a purpose-filled life.

When David stood against the giant Goliath he was, on paper, a "no-hoper".

- Goliath seemed powerful and David seemed weak.
- Goliath seemed impenetrable and David seemed indefensible.
- Goliath seemed huge and David seemed small.

There was one major difference – Goliath was confident in himself, but David was confident in God.

Today there are still "giants" in our lives and our land to overcome. They can seem powerful, impenetrable and huge, whilst we can feel weak, indefensible and small.

Are we still confident in God? Is He still a giant slayer?

Giants in our lives

Personal addictions, obsessions and fears can limit our victory. As a former sufferer of some mild obsessive-compulsive disorders I believe we can be free of anything and in Christ we can overcome any giant. If you bring your giants into the light and seek help, you can get victory.

What are your giants? It's time to defeat them.

Giants in our land

In society we face an increase in overt sensuality, an acceleration of violence and gun crime and a disregard for life through abortion. We see damage to property and social problems such as suicide, debt and despair in growing proportions. On top of this we face a lack of reverence for God. There are giants in our land and yet God is still in charge. He is Lord and one day everyone will bow to Him. If we look to Him then we can still change the world.

What are our giants? In Jesus we can defeat them.

34

The Dying Thing

On 27th September 2002 Susan and I entertained our next-door neighbour and five of her friends to dinner. They are all over seventy and when they arrived the room was filled with the smell of lovely perfume. I had not realised that they were all widows and during the meal I asked them what were the challenges of living alone. During the next hour we listened to an immensely moving and challenging conversation. They said that if you have loved and lived with someone for over forty years it is the simple things you miss: the small talk, the reflections on the day, the knowledge that they are there, and the sharing of things together. They spoke of aftershave kept, a husband's toothbrush still next to the basin and of a dressing gown still hanging on a peg. One talked of trimming a rose bush in the garden and finding a string tied around the bush – "I couldn't bring myself to untie it because I knew my husband's hands had tied it." They talked without regret and with huge fondness for men they had loved and who had died.

In the film *Jack and Sarah*, a husband describes the devastation of losing his young wife: "Then it hits you – you remember – and simple things, like the book she was reading, terrify you, because ... she's gone and that's that."

As I write this I am thirty-nine years old. I don't want to die yet and believe that I have many years ahead of me. However, I am ready to die. I wrote a song to be sung at my own funeral that captured all I would want to say to those I love. It seems unfair that we can't speak at the celebration of our own life.

I'm not here
So cry your tears
But don't pray for me any more
What I believed
Built my life on
Now I know it's true

Run the race
Keep the faith
Live your life with passion
And I'll be there
To cheer you home
When your day comes

My eyes have seen
My ears have heard
My mind now understands
What God prepares for those He loves
Please believe me, it's wonderful

Run the Race...

What I have longed for
All my life
To hear Him say, "Well done."
Listen now, I've heard His voice and everything I've ever done,
    everything I've ever known
Has paled into shadow

Keep running
Keep believing
Keep looking
There's something far better ahead

So this dying thing...

We will all die
We cannot stop the process of life. We all get older and everyone dies.

We will all live forever
Everyone will exist beyond this life. The invitation of Jesus is to spend eternity with Him.

We don't need to be afraid
The Christian may not be spared from pain, but they can be spared from the fear of death.

For the Christian death is the gateway into better things
C.S. Lewis writes in *The Last Battle*,

> All their life in this world and all their adventures in Narnia had only been the cover and the title page. Now at last they were beginning Chapter One of the greatest story which no one on earth had read; which goes on forever; in which every chapter is better than before.[1]

Note
1. C.S. Lewis, *The Last Battle* (*Chronicles of Narnia*), HarperCollins, 2005.

35

The Today Thing

The 16th November 2001 was a momentous day for Ray. Thirty-three years earlier, when his youngest son Iain was born, he didn't realise the journey that was ahead. Iain was severely autistic and the stress of home life as well as a full-time teaching job took its toll. Alongside this, Ray and his wife Margaret chose to pioneer care and support for autistic people. This was a difficult task and they were met with opposition, misunderstanding and many obstacles along the way.

Eventually in 1973, after a huge effort, the Cambridgeshire Autistic Society was formed. Next, Ray and Margaret began an extensive fundraising programme that led to the building of a new residential unit for autistic people. Today, as others have carried on the work, twenty-three autistic adults have a safe place because one family made a start. On the 16th November, as we waited outside Buckingham Palace, Ray, my father-in-law, was given an MBE for services to people with autism in Cambridgeshire.

Whether you have an appointment at the palace or not, today will only happen once. You will never get a second chance at this day and it is filled with opportunity, possibility and hope. You will make many choices today that determine its outcome and I urge you to seize the moment.

So what can happen today?

Today you can know God is with you

You will have moments today when you are alone. Remember, not only is Jesus with you, but He is longing to be involved in your life.

Today you can go deeper

Your faith can grow, you can be filled with hope and you can forgive and be forgiven. The One who loves you unconditionally invites you to a new depth in your Christian walk.

Today you can be free

God has no limits and today you can be free from pain, rejection, failure and negative habit patterns. The only limitations today come from you.

Today you can ask for your needs

Whether you need healing, comfort, provision, or closeness, if you ask, the promise of the Bible is that you will receive.

Today a miracle can happen in you

You can take a new step, extend the horizon of your life and realise that anything is possible with Him. You can take a leap of faith.

Today you can encourage another person

You can help someone else, serve another and give to another in a way they will never find out. Today you can be an encourager.

Today salvation can come to your house

People you love can find faith; family can find their way back to God; those who are lost can be found; and you can point someone to Jesus.

Can you say, "I have lived life to the full today"?

Carpe Diem – seize the day.

36
The Hope Thing

During the Korean War many American prisoners of war died of a condition recently described as, "extreme hopelessness". The soldiers were given adequate food, water and shelter. They weren't tortured or physically abused and they weren't hemmed in with barbed wire. However, they were constantly fed bad news and starved of encouragement, good news and hope. It was not uncommon for a soldier to wander into his hut, go into the corner alone, sit down, pull a blanket over his head and be dead in two days. When the survivors were released, very few of them wanted to ring home and upon returning home, they maintained no friendships or relationships with one another. They had lost all hope.

If we lose hope it is easy to become desperate. The tragic root of so many suicides is the loss of hope and the feeling that there is no escape from the present, seemingly bleak, circumstances. Suicide is never the answer and it leaves others with the burden of unanswered questions and an inability to bring closure. There is always another way. If you are reading this and are feeling suicidal, with nowhere to turn, then contact a local church and you will find someone who can help you.

Hope is vital in life. Hope is to believe for something with the expectation of its fulfilment. I love Psalm 71:14 which says, *"But as for me, I will always have hope."* A Christian always has hope, so...

Hope in God's commitment to you

Never underestimate the passion God feels for you.

- You have the hope of salvation.
- You have the hope of God's love – you are loved and will always be loved by Him.
- You have the hope of eternal life. Corrie Ten Boom wrote, when her sister died in a concentration camp, "And so I left behind the last physical tie. Now what tied me to Betsie was the hope of heaven."

Hope in God's Word

The Bible has been banned, burned, ridiculed, and criticised, and yet it prospers. Nicky Gumbel puts it like this: "The Bible is uniquely popular, uniquely powerful, and uniquely precious... it is a manual for life and a love letter from God."[1] God's Word is the truth.

My sister Janice was reading the Bible and came to the account of the thief on the cross. She read the words, "Today you will be with me in paradise" and had a revelation of God's desire for her to know Him. It was a turning point in her life.

Hope in God's promise

He will never leave you or forsake you. He has gone ahead to prepare a place for you. He will be with you to the end of the age. If you call on Him, He will answer you and show you great and unsearchable things. He has a plan for your life and will protect you.

He is a constant companion, the lover of your soul and a light for your path. He is close to you and His promise to you of love, guidance, provision, commitment and hope, will never fail.

Hope in God's forgiveness

In his book, *In the Presence of God*, Francis Frangipane recalls the following story:

The prophet turned to the minister's wife and said, "There was a very serious sin in your past." The woman with her worst fear seemingly coming upon her, turned pale and closed her eyes. The prophet continued, "And I asked the Lord, 'what was this sin that she committed?' And the Lord answered, 'I do not remember'."[2]

God's forgiveness is never deserved or earned. But it is His promise if we repent.

Hope in God's control

Two men were in a museum and they were looking at a painting of a chess game. In the painting, one character looks like the devil and the other looks like an ordinary man who is down to his last chess piece – the king. The title of the painting is "Checkmate". One of the men looking at the painting is an international chess champion and something about the painting intrigues him. He becomes engrossed and transfixed by what he sees. All of a sudden he looks at his friend and says, "We must find the person who painted the picture and tell him that he must change the picture or change the title. I've studied the board and I realise this, that it is not checkmate, because the king still has one more move."

Whatever we face there is hope, for the King always has one more move. God is in control.

Notes
1. Nicky Gumbel, *Questions of Life*, Kingsway Publications, 2001.
2. Francis Frangipane, *In the Presence of God*, New Wine Press, 1994.

37
The Children Thing

During a conversation with his seven-year-old son, a friend of mine was explaining about the Roman occupation of Britain. He talked about their advancement into Wales and England, but explained that they didn't advance fully into Scotland. The boy said, "Daddy, I know why that happened, it's because of the bagpipes, they make such a dreadful noise." The same family were visiting relatives in Germany and the son looked at his dad as they all sat down to dinner and asked, "Dad, what was it you said you didn't like about the Germans?" Lastly, and my favourite, he once asked his dad, "Have you ever been run over by a combine harvester?"

I love children. We can learn so much from them – their innocence, their honesty and their willingness to ask.

Children are receivers
They know their need to receive. From a newborn baby crying for food, to a young child wanting to be hugged, they know they can't do everything themselves.

Children see and believe
When teaching, Susan occasionally dresses up as different characters to help get a message across. One of her characters is Ettie Macechnie, a kindly old Scottish lady from a highland croft who

owns a "wee farm in Scotland". Many children (and some adults) are completely taken in.

Children are playful

All the time, everywhere, all over the world, children play. I have seen children in Africa play with stones and a tin and still be completely involved.

Children live for the moment

They live each day to the full. They get excited about simple things and become engrossed in getting the most out of everything. You only have to visit a playground to see children thoroughly committed to the moment.

Children look to their parents

Many of us have been to a school play or a children's performance of some kind. Whatever their teachers have said beforehand, there are very few children who can resist scanning the audience for familiar faces and then waving enthusiastically.

Children love learning

...and they do it all the time. They have a natural genius and see life in a different way. Spend any amount of time with small children and you will begin to catch again the wonder of learning and looking at life differently.

Children face issues head on

When I arrived at my Mum's house recently my four-year-old nephew, Ben, who was visiting from Africa and just becoming accustomed to the death of his granddad, looked at me and said, "Grandad's dead."

Children are not self-conscious

They get engrossed in their play. They can be Spiderman or Cinderella, they can talk to their imaginary friend, they can dance or shout their way around the garden without caring what anyone else thinks.

Jesus valued and accepted children. He wanted them to be with Him. More than that, Jesus said to us, *"... change and become like little children"* (Matthew 18:3).

So...

- Be a receiver
- Stop doubting and believe
- Enjoy life
- Make the most of every day
- Keep your eyes on the Father
- Be a learner
- Live with openness and truth
- Please the Lord

38

The Boundaries Thing

When Samuel was young he was an escapologist. Without warning he would disappear and this led to some interesting moments. Once we found him in a barrel of water up to his neck and another time in a bog up to his waist. Then there was the time he disappeared after Sunday lunch to go and spend his 20p pocket money on a ride on the electric horse outside the local Post Office. He was four and the whole family searched with growing anxiety until he was met returning across the village green. Without doubt, God preserved his life on a number of occasions.

At home we had the most fun. He could escape from the garden in a moment and eventually we had to make the whole of our back garden "Samuel proof". It may have looked a bit excessive, but for us it created a place of safety. The boundaries brought security.

Psalm 16 is a fantastic passage in the Bible.

- We can find refuge in the protection of God (v. 1)
- We can know security in our relationship with God (v. 2)
- We can receive inspiration from the people of God (v. 3)
- We can show gratitude for the provision of God (v. 5)
- We can live fulfilled and safe in the plan of God (v. 5)

Then we come to verse 6:

> "The boundary lines have fallen for me in pleasant places;
> surely I have a delightful inheritance."

So the boundary thing...

Boundaries release our potential

God's plans are the best for us. We can reach our potential and live a fulfilled, successful, dynamic life as we live within His boundaries. We may not have everything we want, but He will ensure we have everything we need.

Boundaries bring security

They provide protection and keep predators out. All of us are more secure when we know the boundaries. When we instigate accountability and openness, because of our desire to live in God's boundaries, we position ourselves in a secure place.

Boundaries bring discipline

With boundaries, we learn to live within our limits and be structured and efficient. Boundaries can feel restrictive, but in the long run they liberate us. Grace tells us we are loved and forgiven and cannot earn God's mercy. Boundaries tell us that we choose not to take this grace for granted.

Boundaries bring joy

They help us to live an ordered, non-chaotic life in which we can know peace and fulfilment. This is God's plan.

The Bible says as we live within His boundaries we will know "... *a delightful inheritance.*"

39

The Money Thing

Leading up to our wedding Susan and I naively gave away our savings and put a tent and sleeping bags on our wedding list. This was in response to the life of Abraham who was called to leave everything and live in tents. Six weeks before we were married we had nowhere to live and began a fascinating journey. A family approached us and lent us an oak panelled flat for "a price we wanted to pay". I can still see my Grandma looking at my Mum as she looked round the flat and saying, *"Eee, Brenda, for people of our station!"* Following this we lived with a family and then rented a house before being offered it for "what we could afford". The owners then left almost all of their furniture for free and the journey continued. We now live in a four-bedroomed house in a pleasant suburb of Nottingham and when we moved in, God reminded me of the early days when we trusted Him, gave away what we had and set out.

So many stories have followed of living by faith, giving and receiving, cheques in the post, not needing to buy any clothes for the boys until Samuel was seven and learning to be content with little and with much. People have blessed us with support for my music albums, gym memberships and our holidays. We are blessed and have nothing to complain about.

So do these kind of things just happen to some people? I don't believe so.

Money is a massive issue in life. What we do with it, how we feel about it, how we react to those who have more of it than we do, are all vital responses. Jesus spoke about money on many occasions and the Bible gives clear directions regarding how to deal with money.

So, this money thing...

Don't love it

> *The best things in life are free, but you can give them to the birds and bees, I want money (that's what I want) ... I want money, I want lots of money, In fact I want so much money, give me your money, just give me money.*[1]

Jesus said, *"You cannot love God and money"* (Matthew 6:24). Money is not evil, but to love it is. We are surrounded by material things and the desire to have more, better, trendier and nicer things is prevalent. Contentment is forgotten and the pursuit of more money is lived out. We have bought a lie that says money brings happiness and having more is the goal in life.

Do be careful with it

We are all responsible for how we deal with the money we have. To be responsible in budgeting, not borrow too much and avoid credit wherever possible is a life choice. If you are in a mess, seek help (see www.creditaction.org.uk) and then live differently. I believe more and more in using cash wherever possible, in aiming to be generous and in expecting God to intervene.

Don't forget to give it

To give is to be like Jesus. He said that it is more blessed to give than receive. How should we give?

I believe it's vital to...

- Tithe – 10% of all our income before tax to our local church
- Give offerings – above our tithe to anywhere we chose
- Give to the poor – above and beyond tithes and offerings to those who have less than us
- Be sacrificial – to occasionally go without so we can give

If you look at how you spend your money it will reveal what is most important to you. For us, the church, our children's education and buying our home stand out, what about you?

Do live without it

If you are a multi-millionaire, great – you have been blessed so you can be a blessing. To go without is still possible for you too.

Ask yourself the following:

- Is there anything I couldn't give away if challenged?
- How important is it for me to have money?
- Am I content, or do I always want a bit more?
- Do I live to give?
- Do I expect a certain standard of living?
- Am I willing to lay down everything if He calls me to?

Do believe to be blessed with it

God has promised to meet our needs according to His glorious riches. He is able to do abundantly more than we can ask or imagine. If you sow, you will reap. God says,

> *"Test me in this ... and see if I will not throw open the floodgates of heaven ... "*

(Malachi 3:10)

Paul said,

> "I have learned the secret of being content in any and every situation, whether well fed or hungry, whether living in plenty or in want."
>
> (Philippians 4:12)

By the way, we got the tent and still use the sleeping bags!

Note
1. *Money (That's What I Want)*, words and music by Barry Gordy Jr. and Janie Bradford, performed by the Flying Lizards.

40
The Running Thing

My son Tom found a website where you can create your own logo on a t-shirt. In a moment of enthusiasm I asked him to design me something to wear at the gym that would talk about my faith. When it arrived, it said on the back of the shirt in large black letters, "I'm following Jesus, who are you following?" The next day, as I stood in the changing room at the gym, I had a crisis of confidence. What would people say? Why did I have this idea? How could I face my son if I never wore the t-shirt? I put the shirt on, felt compelled to walk to the front running machine, and ran for thirty minutes, realising that maybe fifty people behind could read the directly worded message.

Completely self-conscious, I wore the shirt for many visits, and although I never had a conversation directly because of it, I was deeply challenged by it. When the shirt was ruined due to an unfortunate "accident" with paint I was, to be honest, delighted.

I love running and aim to jog 4–5 times a week.

We all run in life.

What do you run after?

Things?

We all need a home and we all need food and clothing. Whether rich or poor, we all must be wise stewards of what God gives to us. Material things aren't wrong – but to run after them is.

Money?

Bank statements reveal our passions and priorities. Jesus said, *"Where your treasure is, there your heart will be also"* (Matthew 6:21). Money is not wrong – to run after it is.

Pleasure?

We live in a pleasure seeking generation where people demand their "rights", strive for "me time" and where fast food and every kind of entertainment abound. Pause and ask yourself, "Do I need a 'pleasure moment' to find happiness? Am I restless unless I am doing something or going somewhere? Am I content?" Pleasure is not wrong – to run after it is.

Success?

John Ruskin said, "When a man is wrapped up in himself he makes a pretty small package." To have little can be hard to cope with, but to have abundance can be even harder. Success is a drug that can lead to self-dependence and disaster if our character does not keep pace with our achievement. Jesus said, *"He who is least among you all – he is the greatest"* (Luke 9:48). Success is not wrong – to run after it is.

The race

Paul the apostle, near the end of his life, said, *"I have fought the good fight, I have finished the race, I have kept the faith"* (2 Timothy 4:7). Jesus has a race for each of us to run and to run His race is the purpose of our lives.

Live for a higher goal, God's "well done" and refuse to be distracted by a temporary crown or pleasure.

You have one life – run for Him.

41

The Finishing Thing

Billy Graham wasn't the only young preacher filling auditoriums in 1945. Many believed Bron Clifford to be the most gifted and powerful preacher the Church had seen in centuries. He preached to audiences of thousands and at twenty-five had touched more lives and set more attendance records than any other preacher in American history.

Most of us have heard of Billy Graham, but what about Bron Clifford, what happened to him? By 1954, Clifford had lost his family, his ministry, his health, and then his life. Alcohol and financial irresponsibility led to him leaving his wife and their two Down's syndrome children. He died at thirty-five years old of cirrhosis of the liver and was buried in a cemetery for the poor.[1]

In my twenty-one years as a Christian I have watched people whose lives have been changed by Jesus leading to incredible transformations by His grace. I have also watched as many have lost their way, gone back on their commitment and left behind their passion for Jesus.

In the Christian life it is not how you start that matters, it is how you finish.

How can we finish strong?

Realise our frailty

We are all capable of moral failure, pride, materialism and self-deception. Without Jesus we will never make it. People say Christianity is a crutch for weak people. Well, I am weak and I need Him.

Fix our eyes on Jesus

Lean on Him, depend on Him, long for Him and throw yourself on Him.

Stay in the Bible

Read it, meditate on it, confess it, believe it and live it out.

Stay close to a friend

Find someone who loves you enough to tell you when you are wrong or making mistakes.

Stay away from inappropriate relationships

Be accountable, have clear guidelines and never compromise.

Stay alert to the enemy's tactics

To get to the finishing line involves a battle, but we can make it.

Will you commit yourself, from this moment, to focus on the finish line; to run not a short sprint, but a marathon. With His help you will cross the finish line and hear His words, *"Well done, good and faithful servant."*

> *Finish Strong*
> So many lost, casualties on the journey
> Some who once ran strong, now gone, where did they go wrong?
> And how we need His grace, how we need His strength
> Please carry me

Tragedies on the road, on the journey
Some who turn and choose another path and lose their way
And oh, without Your grace we can't make it on our own
Please carry me

To finish strong, to not lose the way is my greatest desire
To speak Your name with my final breath will be my finest hour
Please don't let me run if I've not learned to walk
Don't let me shout if I've not learned to talk
I never want to leave the way

It's not how you start, how fast you run, but finish the race
It's not if you win, if you try, but pass the test
Your grace it helps us stand, we finish in Your arms
Please carry me

Don't give me riches, don't give me poverty
Give me my daily bread
Don't give me fame if it means I will lose You
I long, I crave, my passion – to finish strong

If you've lost your way, lost your faith, lost your hope
Don't know where you are, what went wrong, can't find
    the way home
His grace is enough, His love still stands. He'll carry you[2]

I'll see you at the finishing line.

Notes
1. Steve Farrar, *Finishing Strong*, Multnomah Books, 2000.
2. Lyrics copyright © David Hind, 2003, from the album, *Painting a Picture*, Authentic Media, used by permission.

42

The Reminder Thing

We all have a tendency to forget what is important in life, so here are forty-two bits of hindsight:

1. You are welcome at God's operating table
2. Make memories
3. Rest is the promise of God
4. Miracles are still promised today
5. The Father accepts you
6. When you wrestle with God you walk differently
7. You can have a second chance
8. Sex after marriage can get better and better
9. You can be a great parent
10. Your faith can grow
11. What will people remember about you?
12. God loves you
13. If you want to change the world, you must never give up
14. You don't need to have an affair
15. To honour is a decision, not a feeling
16. There is more of Him
17. Suffering will lead to comfort
18. Loyalty is a Jesus thing
18. Men are great

20. Worship is a privilege
21. Carry your burdens and pray
22. Teenagers are brilliant
23. Above all things, we need Jesus
24. You can have a fantastic marriage
25. Lost people matter to God
26. To serve is to be like Jesus
27. Keep worshipping and be "low maintenance"
28. You don't have to lose your virginity until marriage
29. Words have incredible power
30. You can be a fantastic parent
31. First steps are important
32. We are the fragrance of Christ
33. It's time to defeat your giants
34. Death can be the gateway into better things
35. Anything can happen today
36. Always have hope
37. Children are amazing
38. Boundaries bring security
39. Money matters
40. You have one life – run for Him
41. I'll see you at the finishing line
42. Remember the important things

We hope you enjoyed reading this New Wine book.
For details of other New Wine books
and a range of 2,000 titles from other
Word and Spirit publishers visit our website:
www.newwineministries.co.uk